NatWest Small Business Bookshelf

This series has been written by a team of authors who all have many years' experience and are still actively involved in the day-to-day problems of the small business.

If you are running a small business or are thinking of setting up your own business, you have no time for the general, theoretical and often inessential detail of many business and management books. You need practical, readily accessible, easy-to-follow advice which relates to your own working environment and the problems you encounter. The books on the NatWest Small Business Bookshelf fulfil these needs.

- They concentrate on specific areas which are particularly problematic to the small business.

- They adopt a step-by-step approach to the implementation of sound business skills.

- They offer practical advice on how to tackle problems.

CW01065004

The author

James W. Dudley is a leading expert and consultant on international business. He is a well known business author and commentator on international management. He lectures widely throughout Europe and the USA. He is a visiting lecturer to The Cranfield School of Management and to colleges in the South East of England.

He has had an extensive business career working in Europe, Africa and the Far East for such companies as Eden Vale, Nabisco and Boots. He was Regional Director for Northern Europe for Boots before setting up his own management consultancy practice – James Dudley Management. He is also a special advisor to Welbeck Golin/Harris Communications, one of Europe's leading marketing communications companies.

Other titles in this series

A Business Plan
Book-keeping and Accounting
Exporting
Franchising
Hiring and Firing
Managing Growth
Selling
Small Business Survival
Starting Up

This book is dedicated to my daughters
Susannah and Sarah.

NatWest Small Business Bookshelf

Exporting

James W. Dudley

Pitman

Pitman Publishing
128 Long Acre, London WC2E 9AN
A Division of Longman Group UK Limited

First published in Great Britain in association with the National Westminster Bank,
1989

British Library Cataloguing in Publication Data

Dudley, James W.
  Exporting. – (NatWest small business bookshelf)
  1. Exporting by Small and Medium-sized firms –
  Manuals
  I. Title   II. Series
  658.8′48

ISBN 0-273-03099-X

Typeset, printed and bound in Great Britain

Contents

Preface

There has never been a better time to explore the export opportunity. With an estimated £5.4 billions worth of untapped business Britain's smaller firms have a lot to go for. The amount is so significant that a vast new network of DTI, EC and private sector support is emerging to hold the hand of the new exporter.

So, if you have never exported before or are reading this book to learn more about the subject, your timing could not have been better chosen. The coincidence of booming North American and Far Eastern markets, the gradually expanding opportunity in Europe's Single Internal Market and the network of support come together to make export-led growth for your business a real and major priority. No book on small business exporting has so far opened the pages on the new wave of opportunities, initiatives and enterprise programmes that are emerging.

Exporting for the smaller business is no mere 'hand me down' of big company strategies. It is a subject in its own right. For not only do smaller firms have to find strategies to market their products; they need to do so under many constraints, such as finding people, resources and finance to match their goals with skills, products and funds.

This book then is a serious work. Its authority as a working guide is based on extensive research, the wisdom of many people successful in small business exporting and providing assistance for exporters. It brings too the experience of this author as a management consultant, lecturer and seasoned internationalist.

James W. Dudley
April 1989

Acknowledgements

I offer my grateful thanks to all those people and organizations who provided valuable contributions, their wisdom and technical assistance, without whom the task of writing this book would have been much more difficult:

Sir Charles Villiers, Chairman of British Steel Industries and Small Business Research Trust; John Parsons, CBE, of the Small Firms Committee, BOTB and Chairman of Time and Data International; Andrew Langsley, Association of British Chambers of Commerce; T. Ian Weatherhead, Peter Bishop, Bill Bailey and Clare Burton of The London Chamber of Commerce; Roger Taite, Birmingham Chamber of Commerce and Industry; H. W. Bailey, British Exporters Association; Nicholas Batchelor, *Financial Times*; the National Westminster Bank plc; Departments of The DTI Commission for the European Communities in London; and The Queen's Award Office.

1 Why export?

The change factors □ Europe post-1992 □ The advantages of exporting □ Exporting – the core of an international marketing strategy □ What is exporting?

There are two types of company in Britain today, those which have international vision and those without it. It comes as no surprise, therefore, when research shows internationally oriented firms doing a lot better than those which are not. Yet the irony is that they tend to out-perform their more myopic rivals in the home market too.

Successful firms are set apart from the less successful by the cultural and attitudinal characteristics of those who lead them. As John Parsons, CBE, Small Business Representative of the BOTB Committee and Chairman of Time and Data Systems International, says in describing successful firms:

'It is attitudes such as commitment and enthusiasm from the top of the organisation for exporting, with direct involvement of senior management who have global vision ...'

A commitment to exporting is a clear sign that a company is led by progressive and visionary entrepreneurs. It demonstrates all those qualities needed for the enterprise of the 1990s to meet the challenges of a rapidly changing business environment – one which will be turbulent, more competitive and global.

The change factors

If Europe's Community is to become a Single Market, then such is the world's destiny. Despite the barriers of trade imposed on imports by many countries to cocoon their national companies, the trend is towards freer trade. There are few places in the world where you will not find a high proportion of foreign-made products competing alongside local goods.

So why is a global market place evolving? Sir Charles Villiers, Chairman of the Small Business Research Trust, stated recently:

'In this century there has never been such a combination of business dynamics – we are all now change driven.'

He gives five reasons for the evolution of the global market place.

1. American multinationals.
2. The rise of business skills and purpose of Japan.
3. The information technology revolution in communications.
4. 'Glasnost' in the USSR, opening opportunities previously closed.
5. The formation of a Single European Market in 1992.

A competitive tide is racing over a beach of new opportunities, yet it will be the progressive internationally oriented businesses who will swim. Those 'stuck in the mud' will be swamped or sucked in by those fierce competitors who will cut them from the supply chain altogether.

Firms have yet to realise that many of their customers are already buying from the international market. Still many more are failing to notice the sea-change of industry restructuring as firms shape up for the challenges ahead. Yet the unknowing will not notice that their customers and competitors, and even their suppliers, are changing as a result of the new industry structures.

If companies fail to find new markets and opportunities they will be unable to build the essential foundations for the new competitive environment, namely scale economies, well funded research and development, an organisation built around the right kind of modern-thinking management and skilled staff. Beyond 1992, there will be few worthwhile defendable niches in which to shelter from the fierce forces of national and international competition. Firms unable to draw on an international marketplace for sales and new business opportunities will simply not have the economies of scale to fight off fierce attacks by their more internationally oriented competitors who will drive down prices and margins.

The economic forecast for Europe over the next five years predicts that:

- Demand for products and services will increase.
- Competition will intensify.
- Prices will be driven downwards.
- Industry will restructure in favour of those progressive enterprises who are the best users of management and resources.

If you are sceptical, then believe that the combined forces of twelve European Community governments are dedicated to creating policies *which will make this happen*. The Single European Act signed in 1987 was not a decision made without the full realisation of its consequences. It was signed out of necessity to make European industry more competitive and fitter to match the challenges from the rest of the world. The much-heralded 1992 phenomenon is a survival strategy – it is not an option.

Europe post-1992

No doubt you will have heard about the Single European Act and the creation of the Single Internal Market by the end of 1992. This, if you have not grasped its meaning, is the most important event in European history since the EEC was formed in 1958. Its basic aims are to restimulate the collective economies of the EC member states through creating a Single Market which will allow a free movement of:

- goods and services
- people
- money

throughout the EC. Reinforced by legal instruments and the European Court of Justice, EC policy is directed at:

- Making firms competitive.
- Stimulating economic activity.
- Preventing government-contrived distortions to trade which prevent free and fair trade.

To this end the Single Market will be created around:

- Removing trade barriers.
- Harmonising product standards.
- Opening competition (for both private and public procurement).
- Promoting technology.
- Encouraging small businesses.
- Enacting economic, social and environmental legislation to ensure the benefits are shared by all states.*

So what does this mean for the small- to medium-sized business?

First, business is going to be more competitive in the EC. Many of the hidden barriers to trade which have protected smaller businesses both here and in the other Community countries will go, such as:

*From *1992 Strategies for the Single Market*, James W. Dudley. Kogan Page, 1989.

- Public procurement contracts to local firms.
- State subsidies and hand-outs.
- National product standards as a barrier to trade.
- Discriminatory taxation and VAT.

This will provide opportunities for progressive companies, yet will create threats to those 'stuck in the mud' firms.

Take the example quoted by Charles Batchelor in *The Financial Times* (14 March 1989):

> 'A British company, a supplier of dustmen's overalls to a local authority, faces losing a lucrative contract. The local authority has learnt that an Italian company can supply overalls 40 per cent cheaper'

Under EC law the local authority cannot discriminate between a British and an Italian firm!

In Brussels and around the Community more than 80 committees are evolving new health and safety and environmental regulations. These too will affect your business. To cut out discriminatory product standards they will have to be harmonised and this involves change. It also involves cost for firms. If you have to amortise those costs across a small domestic market you will be at a disadvantage to those enterprises selling across several EC markets.

The advantages of exporting

All too often we hear that exporting is vital for our balance of payments – particularly as we have been in the red for some time. Yet what so many people forget is that it is just as important for British firms to occupy the centre ground of their domestic markets to satisfy home consumption as it is for them to generate exports, in solving a balance of payments problem.

Historically it has been the absence of exporting which has been responsible for the demise of many domestic companies – the reason being you need an export market to become both competitive in price and cost at home. You need the global market to develop your expertise and innovations. Larger markets are a must for firms developing products which are to be competitive in terms of function, quality and cost.

The advantages of exporting, therefore, are:

- A larger marketplace against which to fund research and development, capital investment and marketing costs.

- A gradually expanding market opportunity against which to plan business development.
- A portfolio of markets against which to absorb the temporary shocks of interest rate hikes or sudden falls in demand at home.
- The facility to trade in a number of foreign currencies to smooth the effect of foreign exchange fluctuations on your imported materials and capital equipment (whether you buy them direct or not).
- The benefits of cross-fertilization of ideas as you tackle different sets of customer needs and expectations around the world.
- The demonstrated vision and commitment shown by management to which much importance is attached by investors and analysts (important if you are on your way to being listed).
- The opportunities which having an international business provides in securing licences from other firms or for other forms of collaboration (both inward and outward).
- The attractiveness of the enterprise as an employer – particularly for management grades.

Exporting – the core of an international marketing strategy

Exporting is one of several strategies for creating an international business (see Fig. 1.1). It is more often than not the central feature of an enterprise's overseas expansion – and will always be part of most companies' international business.

Compared with other strategies for becoming international, export has three key advantages, namely:

- It is generally accepted as a lower risk method of expansion.
- It permits a company to grow organically – thus allowing it to exploit its core technology, production, human resources and experience in making and marketing its products.
- It enables business to build networks of contacts around the world through which collaboration strategies, joint ventures, acquisitions and other investment opportunities can be identified, located and exploited.

It is in this last respect that enterprises with vision and wisdom really benefit. From the boardroom the rest of the world is a distant and foreign place – and without some knowledge of different markets, their opportunities and peculiarities, it is difficult both to decide upon and to locate potential acquisitions, joint venture opportunities and so on. Once you are trading abroad your knowledge multiplies as does your 'grapevine' from your network of contacts (Fig. 1.1).

6   Why export?

Options for international strategies:

1. *Exporting*: Building new markets from a limited-number production base.
2. *Joint ventures*: Entering a corporate arrangement with foreign partners to exploit foreign markets jointly.
3. *Acquisition*: Buying foreign companies to secure a presence, market and organization – or buying a UK firm with foreign bases and facilities.
4. *Licensing*: Exporting technology.
5. *Setting up subsidiaries*: Moving marketing and production off-shore.

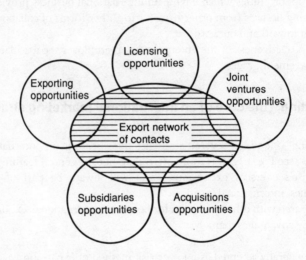

Fig. 1.1 Options for international strategies and the export network of contacts. *Copyright James Dudley Management 1988*

Exporting then not only provides a relatively low-risk way of building an enterprise through the building blocks of its skills, products and resources – it creates opportunities for other international strategy options.

The message is: Exporting is a core element for building your business both at home and abroad. It should be central to your enterprise expansion strategy. It helps protect your home business by making it more cost effective and provides greater opportunities in which to invest. That is why firms engaged in exporting do a lot better than those which are not.

What is exporting?

Exporting involves finding foreign markets, setting up marketing organisations, developing business within those markets, making transactions, physically shipping goods to markets, managing the movement of documents and managing the processes of getting paid.

There are three basic forms of exporting:

Passive exporting, i.e. where a firm receives and meets orders from abroad without any active participation in securing them. This process is stimulated by foreign enquiries which might be the result of buyers seeing goods on sale in the UK or advertisements or articles in the public or trade press, or of buying organisations actively seeking out products on behalf of foreign buyers.

Intra-firm exporting, i.e. where firms export raw materials or components to overseas factories and installations.

Active exporting, i.e. where a company actively pursues an export strategy in terms of finding and developing markets.

To be successful in exporting you need to:

- Understand the different business environments in which you operate.
- Select and prioritise markets.
- Find the right products.
- Set up the right marketing and sales organisation.
- Find and obtain government support (grants, subsidies, contacts).
- Find appropriate promotional strategies.
- Price your products correctly.
- Set up some form of internal organisation.
- Understand the processes of shipping, documentation, insurance.
- Know how to negotiate contracts and get paid.

Above all,

- Know how to create an export strategy.

This book aims to help you do just that.

2 Developing an export strategy

The nature of the market □ Competition □ Export marketing strategy □ The difference between sales orientation and marketing orientation □ Marketing strategy framework

The single most difficult constraint for small firms entering into export is financing marketing costs and distribution networks.

Most of the available texts make the assumption that the small business merely seeks to achieve a marginal share of any markets they intend to enter and can thus get away with low marketing investment and leave distribution to third parties. Unfortunately this assumption is sorely flawed. It ignores both the issues of competition and customers.

If you cannot achieve more than a marginal share of market you will not generate enough enthusiasm from your channels of distribution to handle your product. At best you can expect a series of *ad hoc* deals; at worst you might face stock returns and a ruined opportunity. If you fail to secure a market position the gradually expanding export opportunity turns into an unprofitable and time-consuming business.

So, why not tackle the issues of what resources and finance you need to secure a profitable market position first, and then find strategies that enable you to overcome any hurdles which will stand in your way? By approaching the strategy this way you may well discover that not only do you find ways of overcoming resource constraints, but you also find ways to endow your export project with a number of factors likely to make it successful.

How do we approach the problem?

First ask yourself what are the factors which will be critical to the success of your export project. These will include:

- **The nature of the market.**
- **The size of share you need to become profitable in terms of cost and price.**
- **The channels of distribution.**
- **The competition.**
- **The type of consumers at whom you are aiming your products and their buying habits.**

- **Your own strengths and resources compared with the needs of the market.**

The nature of the market

Figure 2.1 describes the different phases of market development. The curve shows the stages through which markets evolve from the introductory stage through growth to maturity and eventually decline.

The interesting feature of market development is that as it matures the costs of entry become higher and marginal products find it more difficult to survive. If you read off the features of the market from the curve you can see how you will need to consider both your cost of entry and how you can expect the market to evolve. Obviously some markets mature more slowly than others, so you will need to look closely at the pace of market development. You can also see how flawed the argument is for taking a marginal position, for at whatever stage the market is, the marginal position does not work. At introduction and early growth stages your strategy will imply growing with the market, at later growth and maturity you will either fail to enter the market or possibly fall victim in the shake-out stages.

Your first question therefore is, 'What stage is the market at in its development and how rapid is the pace of evolution.'

The size of share you need

Below a certain share of the market you are not going to become competitive in either costs or price. You need therefore to calculate the minimum level of business you have to attain to enable you to make a reasonable contribution from it.

For this you will need to know how much you will have to sell, how different volume levels affect your costs, the maximum prices you might achieve and the level of marketing, distribution and service costs you are going to need to find.

You will probably have to do this calculation several times over as it will beg of you considerable amounts of information about your potential competitors as we shall see below.

However, do not at this stage start to whittle away at costs to try to make your minimum market share look attractive. The aim of the exercise is to determine the real minimum share of the market you will need to achieve a competitive level of cost and price.

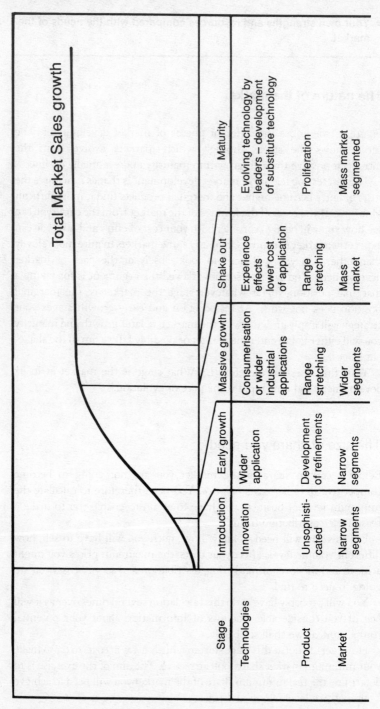

Fig. 2.1 Scheme for determining phase of market development

Competition	Low	Low	Intensifying (band wagon effect)	High cost producers exit market	Dominant – threat of substitutes
Prices	High	High	Lower	Lower	Low
Margins	High	High	Lower	Lower	Medium
Entry strategy	Innovate	Follow early innovators with a point of difference (cost/promotion/ innovation)	Exploit early technology with new ideas/ lower cost products	Find a unique niche	Find a unique niche (cost flexibility unique product offerings)
Entry costs	Low	Low	Medium	Medium to high	High
Market prices					
Target price					
Maximum product cost					
Target market share					

2

Construct a break-even chart as shown in Fig. 2.2 to work out your minimum sales value and then convert this to market share. Then fill in the appropriate boxes on the Table in Fig. 2.1.

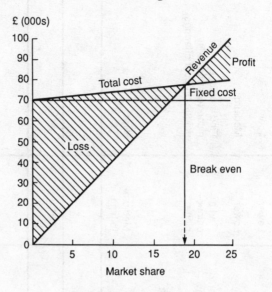

Fig. 2.2 Break-even analysis

Channels of distribution

Your next step is to examine the channels of distribution in your target export market. What stages must your products pass to reach the final customer or consumer? Draw up a model of the distribution channels as they affect your business, along the lines of Fig. 2.3.

Wholesalers	Retailers	Consumers (trade or public)
Nos/% of distribution handled by 5% 10% 20% 50% etc.	Nos/£ % multiples Nos/£ % independents Nos/£ % specialist outlets	Proportion of purchases made by consumers

Fig. 2.3 Distribution channels model

If you examine the distribution channel system you can determine the sort of distribution requirements you will need. Obviously short channel systems where your products are more likely to be bought by businesses rather than end users will require different levels of distribution than for a consumer market dominated by multiple retail outlets. Markets dominated by independent retailers being serviced by wholesalers will again demand a different approach to distribution.

Answer the questions posed in the table regarding the length of the distribution channel system, its features and peculiarities. From these questions we will be able to determine the size of the sales force required to cover the channels of distribution and determine the level of distribution service required.

2

A further point worth bearing in mind concerns the proportion of sales presently passing through major multiple retailers, for this introduces a number of key issues which may determine your choice of decisions later, namely:

- The maximum number of competing brands each multiple will accept – and the minimum turnover of any single brand in the range stocked.
- The propensity of multiple retailers to push their own-label products in preference to manufacturers' brands.
- The attitudes of multiple retailers' buyers to dealings with third party intermediaries.
- The pricing, discounting and service level policies of multiples.

Where the distribution channel system is heavily dominated by multiple retailers, particular attention will need to be paid to your distribution options (see page 148).

Competition

It is too easy to ignore competition at the planning stage, only to find that it presents major problems later.

Entrenched competitors have three major strengths:

- Customer loyalty.
- Knowledge of the market.
- Ability to dislodge a new entrant to the market at lower cost than the cost the new entrant has to invest to gain a foothold in the market.

Yet competitors provide invaluable insights into the market and their very success can help us seek points of entry into the market. Some of the action we can take to analyse competitors is:

- We can obtain a catalogue of all the existing products available in the market sector.
- We can find out the range of prices customers are prepared to pay.
- We can estimate the level of advertising spent by competitors.
- In many cases we can buy or acquire information which will tell us what market share each competitor has.
- We can identify potential segments in the market not adequately catered for by existing suppliers.
- We can examine their advertising to work out their selling points.
- We can look for weaknesses in terms of the products they are offering and the needs and aspirations of customers and users.
- We can determine the nature of the market by looking at their growth and level of product innovation.
- We can seek to establish the pressures on profitability by looking for signs of industry restructuring through mergers and take-overs.

When you analyse the competition it is not only necessary to look at what the competition is offering in terms of products and prices. You need to determine the extent to which it is fragmented on the one hand or controlled by a few dominating companies on the other. It is a fact of life that the structure of channels of distribution in this respect tends to be mirrored by the structure of companies supplying them. If you then look back at your analysis of the 'nature of the market' you will see the restructuring process following the evolution of the maturity curve.

You need therefore to complete the questions in the analysis summary above, namely the level of fragmentation, the presence of dominant companies and the identifiable segments of the market occupied by existing competitors, and look for potential gaps left in the market either because they are ignored by competitors or where their present offerings fall short of customer expectations.

Exporting marketing strategy

Companies which are successful exporters are set apart from those which are not by a single feature of their approach – namely they think *marketing* rather than just sales. It is a fact of life that once you can build regular demand for your products in a few territories your business becomes more profitable and less 'transactions-risky'. As you build up experience in markets you move away from a series of *ad hoc* deals towards building relationships with customers – and enjoy the benefits of regular demand.

The more you know about your markets and your customers the more efficiently you can both plan for and meet their needs. You are better able to plan your production, decide on appropriate contractual terms and focus on planning activities rather than reacting to problems. So, what is an export marketing strategy and how does it differ from a sales approach?

Marketing is about developing demand for products through an understanding of market needs, and creating strategies to exploit them. Selling is about finding customers for products, and inducing them to buy. Whilst selling is a key element of marketing strategy it is not a substitute for it. Sustained demand is the result of a successful marketing strategy – sales are stimulated by selling activities but even the best salesperson in the world cannot sustain demand for products which the market either does not need or does not think it needs.

Marketing strategy then is the process of *developing* a firm's business by *matching* market needs to what the company is good at making and selling, the words 'developing' and 'matching' having been carefully chosen.

Yet one of the biggest problems is in communicating the meaning of the concept of marketing to business people to whom the natural process of doing business is fulfilling their customers' daily orders. The idea that you create 'marketing' for a reasonably successful firm implies that what managers have been doing before is wrong. Herein is the reason which prevents the concept from being accepted.

Most firms which are successful have an inherent marketing capability, whether they recognise it or not. The process of developing a marketing approach to exporting should be based on asking questions about what has made the firm successful to date and how you can use that knowledge to improve performance and expand markets.

It is a strange phenomenon that firms which are very good at their present business often fail to be successful with new products or new markets. More often than not, the reason is as follows:

● That they do not know why they were successful and have no frameworks around which to plan future successes.

Marketing orientation is really no more than a mental attitude which constantly begs questions about markets, opportunities and the hurdles to cross in order to exploit them.

The difference between sales orientation and marketing orientation

The fundamental difference between sales and marketing orientation is that marketing is about *developing demand* and selling is about making *sales transactions*.

To help you decide on whether your approach is sales or marketing in orientation, ask yourself the questions in the following checklist (and tick the appropriate box).

Question	Marketing oriented		Sales	
How far forward do you plan?	Long term (more than 3 years)	☐	Short term (less than 3 years)	☐
How is your market selection made?	Based on analysis of opportunities and priorities	☐	No selection method used	☐
What are your key sales/ marketing objectives?	Develop markets	☐	Weekly/monthly sales targets	☐
How are resourcing decisions made?	Matched to strategy	☐	Minimum to achieve sales objectives	☐
What methods of market entry are used?	Most appropriate for markets selected	☐	No evaluation of options	☐
What are your product policies?	Develop and adapt products to maximize potential	☐	Design and sell home market products	☐
How are channels of distribution selected and managed?	Planned, managed and cultivated to meet marketing strategy requirements	☐	No planning or control	☐
What is your pricing strategy?	Linked to marketing strategy	☐	Based on minimum cost-based sales price/ on deals	☐
What is your promotion strategy?	Planned strategy	☐	None/Left to intermediaries	☐

Marketing strategy framework

Every company is different. Therefore it is extremely difficult to prescribe the right ways of approaching strategy. In order to simplify the main elements of export strategy therefore we examine some of the planning frameworks which are helpful in determining strategy.

Company and environment

In Chapter 3 we will look at the principal factors influencing the business environment. To begin to evolve a marketing strategy for each market it is necessary to look at how your business relates to the business environment – in terms of the shocks and prospects which await you in each market and the strengths and weaknesses inherent in your business.

2

Economic/ demographic/ competitive environment			Social/cultural/ language factors
	Strengths	Weaknesses	
	Opportun- ities	Threats	
Technological change			Political and legal factors

Fig. 2.4 Overlay of the company competitive position on the four key business environment factors

Your basic aim is to use this framework (Fig. 2.4) to find a match between what your firm is best at and whatever success requirements the business environment will force you to meet. You need to assess fully your business strengths and see how these match up to what the market will demand. You then need to look at your own weaknesses and find ways of either putting them right or adapting your strategies to mitigate them.

It is worthwhile taking on board the notion that weaknesses are only such under certain circumstances. You can turn apparent weaknesses to strengths through the way you adapt strategy. In the same way, of course, your key strengths can become major weaknesses if you do not focus your business strategy through them. The next issue examines turning weaknesses to strengths (see Chapter 3).

Strategy focus

One of the critical weaknesses for smaller firms is their relative size and capacity. Yet this weakness can be turned to a major advantage.

The principal differences between large and small firms is that large firms have the capacity to meet the demands of large and broad market segments. They need the scale of large markets to remain successful. To this end they have to develop their markets along the lines of increasing capacity. In so doing, it becomes uneconomical for them to go for relatively narrow niches in markets. They do not have the flexibility to focus on narrow market niches.

The smaller firm on the other hand is much more flexible and capable of attacking these narrower niches profitably – because they can make a profit by sub-optimising large firms. Thus by focusing on specific market segments which should form profitable market niches for you, you can achieve a competitive position against larger firms.

Competitive advantages

The next area of competitive advantage to examine is whether you can use your narrow niche capability either to become a competitive player in terms of cost and price or to meet very specific customer needs. In other words, is what you can offer a cost benefit or something which sets your business apart (products, service, special skills, etc.)?

If you are a low-cost business, focus on that strength. If your firm has something really different to offer, focus on that. Do not try to do both: otherwise either you will lose profits because you let costs rise by trying to be special, or by trying to shed costs you will lose your capability to offer a special product or service.

To deploy your competitive advantages you will need to look for markets in which you can best exploit them – or adapt your competitive advantages to meet market needs.

Framework for the marketing mix

One of the easiest ways of looking at the marketing mix is to divide it up into what business schools call the four Ps (Fig. 2.5).

Now, you might say that this general framework for marketing strategy development applies just as much for the home market as it does for export; in this you would be right – but we can use the same framework to look at some of the issues which are peculiar to our export decisions, i.e.:

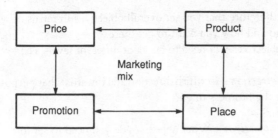

Fig. 2.5 The four Ps

Product:	Which products will be central to our export strategy? What adaptations will need to be made, and what new developments will we need to undertake (see Chapter 4)?
Place:	Where are we going to export our products, and what distribution systems will we need? What sort of sales and marketing organisation will we need? What shipping methods will we need – will we produce in the UK or elsewhere?
Promotion:	Who is our target audience? What methods of promotion are available to reach them, and how will we use them – can we standardise on our UK promotion or will we need to adapt or produce a new campaign (see Chapter 9)?
Price:	What price can we charge? What is the market's price expectation in terms of prevailing prices? What will be the effect on other markets if we differentiate our prices between markets?

The underlying principle of the marketing mix is that each element has a certain interdependence on the others. The place element, for example, is affected by the type of product we will be marketing. The price will reflect function and quality perceptions by targeted consumers. Promotion will communicate the product to its target markets and will be influenced by where and how we choose our products on the one hand, and the value it will create (i.e. price) on the other. To get the most out of each element of the marketing mix, these elements have to be planned so that they work together. The aim is to create synergy.

Objectives

It is all well and good providing frameworks and theories. It comes to nothing if there is no underlying direction and purpose for business. It is essential therefore that you set overall objectives in terms of where you want to go and how you want to get there.

Your objectives will need to be set at different levels, i.e.:

Strategic direction – In which direction and towards what purpose are you intending the business to go?

Strategic objectives – What objectives do you need to set for:

1. business development/products/markets?
2. future revenue?
3. resources/personnel organisation?
4. finance?
5. production?
6. costs?
7. time scales

Planning objectives – Here you will be considering subsets of objectives to achieve your overall strategy objectives:

1. product development projects,
2. new market projects,
3. pricing objectives,
4. distribution/logistics objectives,
5. production targets,
6. promotion objectives,
7. organisational objectives.

Operational Missions – At this level you will be breaking down your planning objectives into sets of operational missions:

- monthly sales targets,
- shipment timings,
- distributor targets,
- promotional campaign targets,
- exhibition targets, and so on.

Projects

One of the key disciplines in market and product development is setting projects. These allow you to cluster work activities to achieve specific end results – for example a new market entry; a new product development;

finding and appointing a new distributor; setting up a collaborative arrangement.

By creating projects and monitoring their progress you separate the day-to-day work of running the business from specific activities which are designed to achieve changes in: business development; ways of doing things; organisational evolution; or financial structure.

The essential ingredients for successful project management are:

- an objective or mission,
- a time scale,
- resources,
- people and skills,
- and above all, a champion to make it happen.

Monitoring activity

An essential part of management involves monitoring activity in terms of:

- Ensuring the scheduled activity takes place.
- Measuring the results.
- Finding reasons for variances between targets and results.
- Keeping experience records to help you to plan future activities.

If you do not know how effective you are in carrying out activities or how effective your activities are in achieving desired results, there is little opportunity to relook at your methods. One of the essential concepts for a modern and competitive business is to understand what is meant by an experience curve.

Research and empirical study carried out in both the US and the UK indicates that the more frequently a business or business unit carries out a set of activities, the better the firm performs them in the future. The more experience you gain, the more effective and less costly activities become, and hence the more successful and profitable the business becomes. To speed up the 'experience effect' you need to monitor your activities so that you can provide the necessary feedback to make improvements to your methods. It is surprising how frequently firms repeat mistakes – this is not a feature of successful firms.

Marketing strategies for export then involve business development rather than transactions. They involve focusing on competitive advantages and deploying your marketing mix to achieve objectives. Business developments should be project-based to separate them from the day-to-day activities. Above all you need to monitor activities to build your experience and improve your effectiveness and ultimately profits.

3   Market environments

Demographic / economic / competition factors □ Social, cultural and language difficulties □ Technology development □ Political and legal factors □ Barriers to trade

No two markets are exactly the same. In fact, within most territories regional differences are very pronounced – even in Britain.

The problem for many business people is deciding which factors will affect their ability to market their products. The aim of this chapter is to provide a framework for examining markets from the point of view of gaining some understanding of the principal factors which will influence trade. The term 'market environment' is used to encapsulate those features in a territory which influence its economic, demographic, competitive, social and cultural, technological and political and legal features – features which will affect all firms competing therein, yet ones which might be used by national governments to favour their own industries and discriminate against foreigners.

This chapter then focuses on two areas, namely:

- Factors which make up a market environment.
- Hurdles countries put in the way of exporters wishing to sell their products to compete with their own national industries.

There are four elements which will influence the environment in which you trade (Fig. 3.1). These are:

- Demographic, economic and competition factors.
- Social, cultural and language differences.
- Development of technology.
- Political and legal factors.

These four elements influence your domestic business and you are no doubt conscious of them at home – even if you do not systematically assess them. In each new market you enter, you will be faced with new sets of these environmental issues. They will of course increase the complexity of running your business. Yet at the same time each national market is influenced by regional and global issues, for example EC legislation, international competition, Third World debt, and so on.

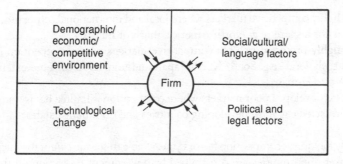

Fig. 3.1 Factors affecting the trading environment

Demographic/economic/competition factors

These three factors influence the size and nature of market segments, the level of purchasing power available and the amount of choice people have in the purchases they make.

Countries differ quite considerably. In rural Third World countries there is only a narrow band of what might be described as middle and upper class households. There are high birth rates and relatively low levels of education. Compare these countries with the more sophisticated Western and Far Eastern countries and you find increasingly wider bands of urban-living middle class segments, higher education levels and in most cases aging populations. The *demographic* composition of markets affects the size of market segments and whether they are enlarging or shrinking.

Economic factors affect the overall health of national economies and the way they are managed by governments. Richer markets are less prone to restrict imports on the grounds that they cannot afford them. Although many, like South Korea and Japan, are very protective of their industries, countries such as Mexico, Sudan and Nigeria have to control the flow of imports because of their limited reserves of foreign exchange.

Economic factors which influence the health of internal economies affect the purchasing power of individuals and firms within a market as well as the ability of a market to pay for its imports. Factors such as 'balance of payments', inflation, gross domestic product, taxation and so on influence both short-term and long-term market conditions.

Competition factors affect the amount of choice customers have – and consequently their expectations in terms of prices and quality. It is a fact of life that the healthier a market is in economic terms, the greater choice available for customers.

Markets can be divided into three categories as far as competition is concerned, namely:

- Highly competitive markets where local and international competitors vie for a share (e.g. North America, much of Europe).
- Highly protected rich but competitive markets where competition is largely local (e.g. South Korea, Japan and until 1992 to some extent West Germany).
- Less developed poor markets where competition is limited but is state-protected e.g. most developing countries and Communist states).

By looking at competition factors you are able to see the extent to which market opportunities are constrained by government protection on the one hand and level of competitive choice on the other.

Social, cultural and language difference

When you begin to expand into new markets you run straight into the problems created by the differences between your home-market and each foreign-market in terms of social norms, culture and languages. The extent to which these will influence the suitability of your products and your behaviour in transacting business will vary from market to market.

The strategy here is to approach social, cultural and language factors pragmatically. The emphasis is on finding similarities rather than differences. Look for market segments rather than generalisation. It is more likely for example that you will find more similarities among say London, Copenhagen and Frankfurt than between Paris and Marseilles, or Berlin and Munich. There will be greater similarities between say 35-year-old male BMW owners than generally between Scots and Scandinavians. There are also more similarities among urban dwellers than among rural dwellers.

The social, cultural and language issues present a minefield for the unwary. If you ignore the issues they will affect your ability to sell your products; if you over-generalise the differences you may never find the right market segments to go for. It is also important to differentiate between those factors which influence the behaviour of buyers in your chosen segments and the customs and norms of transacting your business. If you were selling a product like the 'Walkman', for example, your market segments would be similar all over the world – *but the people with whom you will be transacting your business will have their own norms of behaviour and ways of doing things*. Do not confuse the issues.

Technology development

The pace of technological development poses three problems for the exporter, namely:

- Keeping up with competitive innovations.
- Meeting customer expectations in terms of novelty, function and quality.
- The effects of competitive substitutes on prices and margins.

Whilst you can see the pace of technological development at home and are probably aware of innovations by international competitors, there can be very great differences in individual markets. Again the differences will reflect the type of products you are engaged upon making and developing.

Markets also vary in terms of expectation. If you are selling to Western Germany or Northern America, for example, your customers are likely to expect high quality up-to-date products. The pace of development in those markets is generally higher than in the UK or Scandinavia. Development is often lower in less developed countries and the Latin markets of Western Europe. Yet, as consumers become richer and break-throughs in technology occur, step changes in customer expectation will follow.

The pace of technological development will therefore influence your own choices of markets and the strategies you adopt to keep 'up to speed'. If you lead in your own field (as many small companies do) you should aim at highly advanced markets. If you follow, then you need to select markets where you can compete without 'leading edge' technology.

Political and legal factors

Broadly speaking, political and legal factors have a major influence on individual national markets. The style and quality of governmental management greatly influences the economic state of countries. Legal systems and national norms reflect the ideologies (either political or religious) of the ruling majority in any market. Ethnic and social issues also play a major part.

You can divide countries into a three-by-three matrix (Fig. 3.2).

As a general rule the further towards social advancement and political development a country moves, the fewer the difficulties there are in transacting international trade. Highly autocratic countries tend to be more highly regulated. Yet the greater the proportion of middle class elite within a society, the greater the movement is to open democracy and freedom of choice, open competition and an international outlook.

It is also a regrettable fact of life that countries with dominant power blocks and a narrow band of middle class elite tend to be more arbitrary in their use of power to manage their countries' economies. Competition and poor state management are much greater in highly autocratic, less socially advanced countries, as is exemplified by the Philippines during the Marcos era.

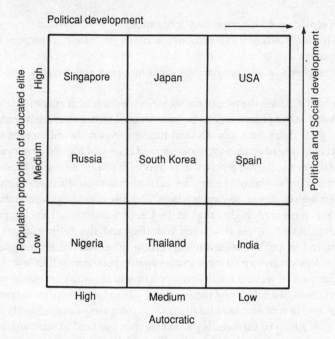

Fig. 3.2 Scheme for evaluating political and legal development.
Copyright James Dudley Management

The key issues to discover in evaluating political and legal issues within a territory are the probabilities of:

Political risk: Warfare, coups, strikes, nationalisation, confiscation of assets.

Economic risk: Currency fluctuations, limitations on available foreign exchange, inflation.

Legal risk: Barriers to trade, discrimination against foreign goods, personnel or assets. Laws of contract and protection of contracting parties.

Barriers to trade

One of the first problems you will face in exporting your products are the myriad hurdles that different countries put in the way of imports. These can be loosely described as tariff and non-tariff barriers.

Countries strive for what is often described a favourable balance of trade. It is believed, if incorrectly, that trade surpluses are favourable and that deficits are unfavourable. Yet where countries have high GDP it is not always to the disadvantage of the country to run a deficit providing it represents a manageable proportion of GDP. A major trade surplus, on the other hand, may have severe disadvantages because, as countries no longer repay their debts in gold, credit is given. If credit is not paid in full this will have an adverse impact on the country with the trade surplus – which is exemplified today by the defaults of many lesser developed countries.

The concepts of free and fair trade are those which describe an enlarged world market in which goods can be traded transnationally without being hindered by tariffs, bans and quotas (free trade) and without creating unfair advantages for its exporters through subsidiaries etc. or hindering imports with barriers (fair trade).

To effect this post-second World War aspiration, a group of major countries convened a conference in 1947 resulting in the formation of one of the most important institutions in the modern world, GATT (General Agreement On Tariffs and Trade). This institution began in 1948 with three principal articles of agreement.

1. A pledge to multilateral trade.
2. An objective to minimise barriers to trade.
3. An objective to reduce import tariffs, quotas and to abolish preferential trade agreements.

Today the organisation has over 70 subscribing nations with a secretariat in Geneva and it is the principal institution for negotiations of free and fair trade amongst nations, albeit the objectives of achieving free trade have been considerably more successful than those for fair trade – even though the failure of the latter in so many respects has mitigated for the former.

Tariffs

Tariffs are imposed on goods crossing national borders by governments on imports or on exports. Sometimes, albeit less frequently these days, countries may collect tariffs on goods being shipped through their country to another – this is called *transit tariff*.

There are three reasons why governments raise import tariffs:

1. To control imports.
2. To raise revenue.
3. To protect local industry.

In controlling trade, tariffs are used to influence demand through the price mechanism. Add duty or tariffs to an imported product's price and it is increased for distribution channels and for the consumer. Hence, for relatively price-sensitive products, demand will contract. For necessities, demand may remain fairly constant but stockists may reduce inventories to protect their cash position and thus imports are reduced. However, one disadvantage regarding tariffs as a means of controlling demand is that governments tend to make them more severe when there is an adverse balance of payments situation and importers will (in pre-empting tariff increases) buy ahead of a budget announcement, thus creating a surge in imports at a time the economy is least able to afford them.

Highly industrialised countries are unlikely to use duty as a major source of income, but favourites like liquor and tobacco tend to be heavily burdened with duty in the majority of countries. Protecting local industry through tariffs is a common reason for instituting a tariff on specific goods.

In lesser developed countries the need to protect local industry is important in helping a country build up its industrial infrastructure. There are no tariffs on trade between member states in the EC – although duty rates on alcohol have tended to be discriminatory and will remain so until duty is harmonized across the EC in the mid 1990s.

Types of tariff

There are basically two types of tariff – *specific* and *ad valorem*.

A *specific tariff*, often called specific duty, is a tariff raised on a specific unit of the goods imported. Such a tariff is easily computed by exporter, importer and customs; thus buyer and seller will have a fair idea of the duty payable on a transaction at the time negotiations are concluded.

A tariff which is calculated as a percentage of the value of a product is referred to as an *ad valorem tariff*. Such tariffs are computed in a variety of ways, even in the same country. The *ad valorem* tariff might be raised on the FOB, C&F, or CIF value of the invoice (see page 127), on the comparative domestic wholesale or retail price, or on the estimated cost of a locally manufactured substitute. Customs are given wide powers to decide the true value of goods imported in order to prevent under-invoicing. However, such powers may be used actually to raise tariffs so high as to prevent importation altogether (see non-tariff barriers).

Non-tarriff barriers to trade

To put it simply, non-tariff barriers to trade are measures taken formally or informally by governments to constrain or prevent imports without resort to punitive tariff barriers. The types of non-tariff barrier most commonly encountered are the following.

Quotas

Quotas are imposed by governments to regulate the inflow of products from specific countries. Where quotas are imposed, it is usual for countries whose products are affected to divide the quota up between exporters. The proportions of the quota share are based on historical sales by existing exporters. This often presents problems for new exporters.

Currency restrictions

A common method used by many lesser developed countries to slow up or stop imports is through currency restrictions. Government departments control the level of imports through their approval or otherwise of each individual import transaction. Unless approval is given, an importer cannot obtain foreign currency to pay for imported products.

Administration of customs

Customs administrations in most parts of the world are endowed with wide-ranging seemingly arbitrary powers – to interpret customs classifications and make charges for duty.

In countries like the US the apparently low tariff schedules are backed up in some cases by American *ad valorem* tariffs which are based on US selling prices rather than on the importer's buying price, resulting in higher duties than is implied from the formal tariff schedule. However, this seems to apply only to a small group of goods.

Another frustrating factor is that caused by frequent changes in customs classification which result in importers being wary about importing certain types of product. Linked to this has been a practice by several lesser developed countries of charging duty on bonded goods at the rate of exchange (at FOB or C&F buying prices) ruling on the date of release from bond. This reduces importers' desire either to buy in bulk to save on price, or to pre-empt quotas and to store them duty-free in bond.

Administration of anti-dumping laws

Protection against dumping is a necessary activity undertaken by governments. However, measures taken to administer anti-dumping regulations are often so punitive as to make even normal importation difficult.

Where a complaint is made, a considerable period of time passes before a final decision is reached; as a consequence there is an interference with normal commerce which discourages further transactions.

Protection of intellectual property

Governments pay great attention to the protection of patents and trade marks of companies operating within their national frontiers. Regulations imposed to protect intellectual property, however, often act as effective import barriers. National patent and trade mark methods are introduced by local companies effectively to prevent the importation of products which compete with theirs.

In some countries, particularly in the US, there is scope within the law for companies to institute a procedure in 'Unfair Competition', so as to obtain an enforceable order which prevents the importation of patented products or goods made by patented processes. This barrier to trade is used to avoid the costs of litigation by some companies.

Health, safety and environmental regulations

Health, safety and environmental regulations defy any form of international standardisation despite the efforts of the World Standards Organisation sponsored by the UN. Amongst its thousands of published standards there is a low proportion of standards which apply to single countries or even regions within countries. The sheer diversity of standards means that some countries are nationally excluded as export markets because companies simply do not find making the necessary adaptations economic. Health and safety regulations, therefore provide a major barrier to imports. It is this area of frustration which has forced much of the Single European Act to harmonise standards throughout the Community, thus ridding it of a barrier to trade.

Food and drug regulations

In 1975 Singapore effectively cut a whole range of marginal food imports, through demanding that all goods should bear labels with certain mandatory information. The most effective block to imports was the requirement that the importer's name and address be printed on the package. Even stickers were not accepted. Hence a number of marginal suppliers found it uneconomic to print special labels for Singapore.

Like health and safety regulations, food and drug regulations are very diverse. In Australia up to 1976 the various states had slightly different regulations, making it very difficult for exporters to accommodate each state's regulations.

Units of measurement, language used, and size of print for mandatory information and so on, make it very difficult for manufacturers to meet every different requirement in all its potential markets, hence constraining international sales. Again the European Commission is in the process of harmonising food and drug legislation within the EC. It will, however, still take some time before the process is completed.

Government procurement

Government purchases influence and constrain in two ways. Firstly, preferences to 'buy local' are imposed on governments by trade lobbies and government's own recognition of its need to support and promote its own country's companies. Secondly, many countries receiving foreign aid do so under trade-related agreements. Hence a government receiving trade-related aid from, say, the United Kingdom will have to offer its tenders to British companies first.

Public procurement policy in the EC makes it illegal for governments and public authorities in any one member state to discriminate against products produced in other member states.

Subsidies

Governments have long learned how to manipulate markets through the application of subsidies. These operate in two ways. Firstly, subsidies on exports make domestic exporters' products price-competitive, thus increasing sales in foreign markets to the detriment of both domestic and foreign competitors. Secondly, governments may subsidise local industry to make them more price-competitive in the local market.

Subsidies may not be direct. They may include subsidies applied for regional development package deals to attract foreign investment. These may be in the form of tax holidays, and subsidising labour costs either directly or indirectly by guaranteeing a minimum wage through social security hand-outs.

Again, governments within the EC are having to withdraw subsidies affecting competitiveness between member states. There are now moves within the Commission to examine the impact of subsidies given by governments to firms for business outside the EC. According to Leon Brittan, the European Commissioner, these too affect internal competition and should, therefore, be withdrawn.

Compulsory preferences

As a means to encourage or force the use of local raw materials and components, some countries insist that a minimum percentage of local products must be used in local production. Sometimes this rule applies to all manufacturers or just to foreign companies. This rule is causing continuous rumblings in the EC and several cases will shortly go to the European Court where member states have refused to accept goods made in other member states from components supplied by external community companies.

Taxes

Taxes are overt means of implementing non-tariff barriers. These constraints on imports are often classed with tariffs in the international discussions on tariffs and trade.

The subtle use of domestic taxes such as turnover tax or selective employment tax, as well as the use of tax rebates on exports and expense allowances when obtaining export business, help favour the exporter at the cost of the importer or non-exporter.

The use of special purchase tax is sometimes applied to charge a higher rate of duty on goods which the local industry can produce. If it is found that a local company can meet an order in the time specified, the import tariff on a competing foreign order is raised.

Import permits

Most governments will or do use import permits in both their short-term and long-term strategy to control imports. Lobby groups, labour unions and industry associations will often solicit governmental intervention to protect new or declining industries.

Restrictive business practices

Companies themselves may help create non-tariff barriers through a variety of practices such as agreeing to assign markets in certain countries to specific companies on an exclusive basis. The practice of price agreements for foreign markets is also a feature of restrictive business practices: these are mostly illegal within markets but are permitted for external markets. Articles 85 and 86 prohibit such activity within the EC by companies within the market.

Trade boycotts, under which domestic distributors, or domestic suppliers as a group, agree to sell domestic products only, will cut off any distributor who handles imported items. Some variations on these means of controlling imported competition include agreements to set up 'private import quotas' or to sell imported products at significantly higher prices.

Other types of restrictive practices include the 'parcelling out of exclusive patent rights in various countries' so that producers can effectively divide up market territories. Whilst this practice is illegal for EC firms operating within the Community, it is not illegal under, say, US law for US firms to transact business this way in their export markets – including the EC!

It is not uncommon to find that some restrictive practices are supported, if not initiated, by governments. National patent and trade mark laws support market allocations. Embargoes, import permits and differential tariffs can be used to implement domestic cartels. There are thousands of such abuses in the EC, all of which are illegal!

Multiple exchange rates

Multiple exchange rates are a method of import control. Governments, by charging importers a high rate of exchange to buy goods from abroad, increase their price, hence reducing demand for non-essential products. In many ways the use of multiple exchange rates is equivalent to the use of tariffs.

Import deposits

A technique used by the UK in the 1960s, and at present in some lesser developed countries such as Malawi and Kenya, is for governments to demand an import deposit to be paid to the National Central Bank by the importer on goods ordered from abroad.

This has two effects. As most importers use the exporter's credit to finance working capital, the importer hopes to sell off much of its imported products before payment falls due. The effect of the deposit is equivalent to the importer having to work from cash, especially if the deposit is 100 per cent. Orders are reduced to the level at which importers are able to meet the deposits. Secondly, the level of inventory is often reduced to below the expected demand so that goods can be sold in advance of delivery and ahead of the time when exporter credits have to be paid.

Local price control machinery

A subtle weapon in the hands of the government is price control. Whereas economists the world over argue as to whether they prevent or fuel inflation, one thing is clear, that as a means of controlling imports, price controls can be more effective than tariffs. If an imported product is price-controlled at below the economic import price, importers will be forced into abandoning products so affected. At least with high tariffs some marginal importing may go on, but if local price regulations force an importer to sell at a loss, there is no legal way in which business can be conducted. Price control may be used in conjunction with other non-tariff methods of controlling or reducing imports.

How to find out about tariffs and import regulations

The DTI has a number of country desks providing information on tariff information, from 'Afghanistan' to 'Zimbabwe'. These are located at 1 Victoria Street, London SW1H 0ET.

4 What to export

Geographic or product orientation □ Four options for export products □ Sell abroad products you make for the UK market □ Adapt your UK products □ Adapt your range to international standards □ Invent products for both home and export markets □ Intellectual rights □ European Patent Convention □ Brand names □ Product liability

Many small businesses fall into exporting almost by accident. You meet a contact abroad, an export customer visits your exhibition stand or foreigners find your product in the UK and make enquiries. Firms are sometimes surprised to see their products in shops abroad as the result of initiatives of an enterprising wholesaler or export merchant. As exports grow and you become more committed to them, conflicting issues come into play.

The problem, of course, arises where you end up with conflicts between manufacturing for your home customers and meeting the demand for export customers, when you know that if you let down either you put your business at risk. The problem is doubly difficult where your export products are not the same as the ones you sell in your domestic market.

Most firms will be faced with decisions about which products should be exported, given the constraints of what the market will accept and the economics of utilising capacity. Your decisions might be summarised as:

- Making what you can sell
  or
- Selling what you can make

Obviously the closer you can get to selling products in your export markets which are similar to those for your domestic markets, the more you can invest in production and reap the value of scale economies.

Unfortunately the world is not like that. Your products for export will need to meet a host of criteria which may be different from those of your home market. The trick, of course, is to find ways of exploiting your technology and marketing know-how in a way which enables you to:

- Make and sell products that your firm is best at, in terms of technology and marketing knowledge.
- Ensure that your business benefits most from focusing on product areas which contribute to the best use of your time, resources and finance.

Geographic or product orientation

It is a feature of European exporting that firms tend to think in terms of geographical markets rather than of a global market for products. The fact that there are some 800 million people in the free world with many similar needs provides considerable opportunities to base an international business strategy on finding similarities rather than differences.

There are basically two types of export markets, namely:

- Those which have broadly common needs and which can be satisfied with products needing only minor adaptations to meet local customs, cultures and regulations.
- Those which are highly 'culture bound' and which need extensive product modification to meet customer demand.

You will, no doubt, be more than familiar with the marketing maxims of consumer or customer orientation. Strategies are rarely successful where customers and competition are ignored. It is not possible to sell products which are far removed from customer expectations and traditional buying habits.

The problem, therefore, is deciding whether to base your strategy on building markets through making and selling products designed purposefully for particular markets – or to find markets which will 'broadly' accept the products you make.

Examine your markets and business strategy on the basis of Fig. 4.1. The broad issues of strategy thus become clear. If you are to achieve the true benefits of scale, making the right decision on orientation will be critical. The *best* strategies are to make specials and develop markets on a geographical basis where they are highly culture-bound. Conversely it is the *worst* strategy to make specials and develop markets using a geographical orientation where there are high similarities between markets.

The effect of adopting *best* and *worst* strategies will seriously affect the profitability of your export strategy because:

- *Geographic orientation* is based on building individual markets. Here you will need to achieve sufficient market share to make it worthwhile

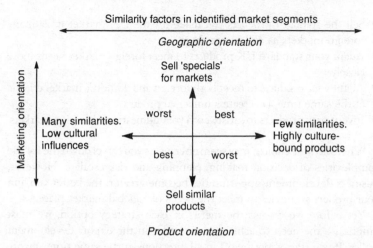

Fig. 4.1 Best and worst strategies based on marketing orientation

to produce specials and to compete in terms of cost and price against local competitors.

- *Product orientation* is based on maximising efficiencies of production scale, enabling you to compete effectively on an international basis with both local and other international competitors. Obviously the greater the extent to which you can dedicate resources to specific products, the greater the extent to which you can enjoy the cost benefits of production.

Choosing *worst* strategies means you will not enjoy the benefits of economic production.

The problem for many firms is that in planning they tend to seek out differences without looking for similarities. The mistake often arises where broad assumptions are made about countries without examining the market segments at which products are aimed. Even within markets with apparently high cultural differences, segments exist which are broadly similar to those of other countries – to wit the success of denim jeans, Walkman stereos, MacDonalds and Filofax, which you will find from Hong Kong to California.

Four options for export products

There are four approaches you can look to as options:

- Sell the standard products you make for the UK market in as many foreign markets as will accept them.
- Adapt your standard UK products to meet foreign market needs more closely.
- Adapt your products to meet both foreign and domestic market criteria at the same time, i.e. create a universal product.
- Invent new products to satisfy both your domestic and foreign markets.

Whereas these choices may seem obvious, as you travel down the list the complexities of decision making, planning and risk escalate. However, business development opportunities become greater, the better you aim your product strategies to meet the needs of a global market place.

Yet before we discuss the merits of each strategy option, we must emphasise the need to achieve some order in the export development policy. If you start shooting off in all directions at the same time you are likely to fail at:

- Focusing on what you are best at in terms of technology and marketing – thus failing to achieve a competitive business development plan.
- Achieving the best returns from the resources you are employing.
- Creating viable market positions for your products – thus putting your business at risk of being unable to sustain its rate of development.

Sell abroad products you make for the UK market

This strategy is often considered as the least expensive. It is more often the first stage in a gradually evolving development of export markets. The advantages are:

- You have products already to hand to offer markets.
- There is no need to retool or spend funds on product development.
- Funding can be focused on marketing investment and production resources.
- There is little need for retraining production and technical staff.

The problems with such a strategy are:

- Your UK products might have only limited appeal to foreign customers because they are designed for British tastes and preferences, making it difficult to justify the costs of marketing and employing special export staff.

- UK product standards may be different from those set by governments in potential markets. (See non-tariff barriers, Chapter 3, and EC product standards harmonisation, below.)
- You might simply encourage foreign competition to develop products based on your ideas which not only shut you out of their markets but motivate them to enter your domestic market.
- Your export arm becomes demotivated through the lack of suitable products to sell.

Your trade-off, therefore, will be in creating additional sales for your existing products and any benefits which accrue through utilising production resources, and the constraints posed by such an approach in terms of providing a base upon which to build markets.

Adapt your UK products

The obvious second option is to modify your UK products to meet the taste and standards criteria of your foreign markets. This will undoubtedly increase your marketing opportunities but will, of course, create the additional costs of making product adaptations and affect your production efficiencies.

The issue here is how to accommodate a product adaptation strategy without over-burdening your production with short runs and in-efficiencies.

The way to tackle this problem is to identify where in the production process your adaptations have to be made. Obviously the further along the process you make them, the greater the level of scale efficiencies you can continue to enjoy (Fig. 4.2).

Your strategy decision should be based on maximising your production economies. You might consider breaking off production at the point at which the export specials begin to impinge on cost efficiencies (see Fig. 4.3). If a bottleneck is created in your production line due to (say) having to meet special packaging requirements, why not spin-off production at

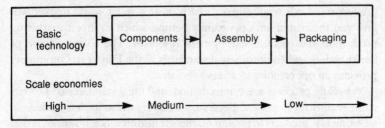

Fig. 4.2 Scale economies tend to fall as you move along the production process

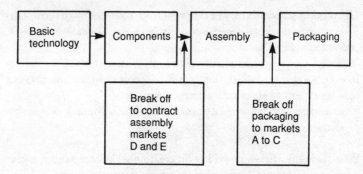

Fig. 4.3 Options to break off production

that stage to your export market and contract out your packaging? In fact you could begin to look at spinning-off production at any point along the production process where specials impinge on production efficiencies. Why invest in additional capacity in the UK to meet the needs of export specials when you can break off production and devolve it to your markets, thus enabling you to invest more in the core stages of production and at the same time reduce the levels of duty or VAT that affect your landed costs as well as providing a better service to your customers?

There is no shortage of contract assembly and packaging companies around the world.

Your decision to break off production will, in financial terms, be based on the real economies of maximising recovery at core stages of production plus savings from duty and shipping costs, less the costs of production abroad.

Adapt your range to international standards

This strategy option is an advance on the one discussed above. What it implies is setting your product standards to international criteria rather than ones based on your UK offerings. In theory, selling marketing and product standards requirements which meet a wider world market will give you the maximum opportunity behind which to invest marketing production and product development resources. The harmonisation of health, safety and environmental standards in the European Community provides an opportunity to achieve just this.

Yet many products are culture-bound, making a standardised product strategy difficult to pursue. Even so, we can return to the suggestions in adapting UK products to foreign markets. The difference, however, is that we can look at adapting the range so that the maximum economies are achieved as far along the production process as possible. If you can achieve standardisation at the points along your process that provide the highest value, then you will enjoy scale efficiencies which can be returned to the market in terms of marketing investment and competitive prices.

Whilst taking this step might involve major strategic investment decisions, there is no reason why your planning should not evolve around this concept. The pressure to conform to basic EC standards may, in fact, push your business in this direction anyway, so if you have to invest in modifying standards, why not do it on the basis of marketing opportunity? This would be a far more positive step than merely conforming to new standards directives.

Invent products for both home and export markets

The larger the market available, the greater the return you will make on your investments in product development. It would make sense, therefore, in selecting development projects, to do so with export intentions in mind. As your range develops for such products, you gain all the advantages in terms of economies outlined in the section above.

In addition to inventing products, you could consider licensing or part-manufacturing products from third parties to add both to your home and export market opportunities. Your position as a company within the EC could well make you an excellent candidate to take on board products from non-community firms as a spring-board for them into Europe.

To do so, however, would mean that you would have to demonstrate your ability to take on their ranges and provide an export organisation for the EC's markets.

Intellectual rights

Once you begin to show your products abroad, you hit the problems of infringing others' intellectual rights or protecting your own. These are:

- Patents on products and processes.
- Copyright designs, packaging and products.
- Brand names.

All three of these areas involve complex legal issues. Whilst you will need to employ specialists, it is important to make the point that an essential part of your initial market entry research involves:

- searches

and

- registration procedures for your intellectual rights.

You need to ascertain whether your targeted markets are ones which accept the principle of:

- the first to register intellectual rights

or

- the first to sell products whose product names and processes are registered.

It is also important to note that in very many countries, patents and brand name registrations can expire through lack of usage. Here you need to take legal advice on how to keep your registrations current, even if you cannot for some reason actively enter a market.

European Patent Convention

In 1978 the European Patent Office was established. Whilst it was a European Community initiative, it includes Austria, Sweden and Switzerland but Denmark, Ireland and Portugal are not signatories.

Through the European Patent Office you can file a patent simultaneously in all contracting countries through a single application. Such an application, if successful, leads to the patent becoming registered in each contracting country and thus providing patent protection enforceable in national courts.

In the next year or two firms will be able to file patents throughout the European Community through the European Patent Convention when this becomes European Community law. This will not only allow you to file a patent through a single application, the European Commission also intends to harmonise rules and establish a common body of law.

Brand names

Registration of brand names is even more complex. All countries have their own criteria, rules and methods of application. It takes a separate set of applications in each country to secure registration. It is both expensive and extremely difficult to get the same name registered in every country.

The Arrangement of Madrid is an agreement covering the international registration of trade marks. This allows a trade mark to be registered in a participating country by a locally domiciled company. The application is then redistributed to each member country via a central bureau. The registration may or may not be accepted under the rules prevailing in each country.

The European Commission is currently preparing the ground for a common system of brand name registration. Again this will not be available for some time to come, in all probability not sooner than 1992.

Product liability

Throughout the world there is an increasing amount of legislation and common law to protect individuals and firms injured by products. The sums involved for compensation are rising astronomically.

The cost premiums for product liability have begun to bite companies in sensitive businesses such as pharmaceuticals. In fact, the cost of such insurance has made some companies think twice about entering the US market. Product liability is an important issue, not just in respect of ensuring that your products are safe, but in the costs of insurance against liability, particularly in the USA.

If your products fall into sensitive areas such as health care, you should double-check the cost premiums attaching to your insurance were you to enter new markets, particularly the USA.

Product liability in the EC is covered under a specific directive, which will be interpreted in much the same way in all member states.

5 Where to export

Research methodology □ Assessing market size □ Assessing potential demand □ Commissioned research □ Commissioning customer research □ Government support for research □ EC support for small to medium sized enterprises □ Government/ private network initiatives into active exporting programmes

The process of market selection is crucial if time and energy are to be expended on fruitful opportunities. Today most people travel abroad and are quite familiar with the differences in language, culture and tastes in different countries.

Probably they are less aware of the overt and hidden barriers to trade, the way distribution channels are structured, and the availability of advertising and promotion and the legal issues surrounding them. Deciding where to export will call for a knowledge and understanding of different potential markets. It will require you to find realistic answers to the following questions:

- Where will my products sell best?
- What barriers are there to prevent my products being imported or to tax them out of the market?
- What sort of competition will my products be up against?
- What sort of distribution network will I need?
- How will I be able to promote my products?

It will be the answers to these fundamental questions which will set you on course to finding markets and prioritising them.

More specifically, prioritisation decisions need to be made on the basis of good and reliable market information. Much of this can be done from information available in the UK from libraries, Chambers of Commerce, government departments, EC sources, banks and trade associations.

A good way to approach your prioritisation of markets is to evaluate a large number and select an initial short list of candidates for greater depth of evaluation. Your first stage of work for selecting a candidate list from a larger number of markets will involve:

- Investigation of presence of overt or hidden barriers to trade.
- Some sort of initial assessment of market potential.

- Recommendations for the mode of entry (e.g. through distributors, joint marketing arrangements, licensing, etc.).
- Description of competitors.
- Brief evaluation of competitors' products.
- Outline of trade channel structures.

This survey will enable you to list your marketing opportunities on the basis of:

- Market potential.
- Mode of entry.
- Level of competitor intensity.
- Possible segment opportunities not occupied by competitors.
- The limitations of channels of distribution.

Market potential

		High	Medium	Low
Accessibility	High	Holland Belgium	Eire	Kenya
	Medium	USA Germany	France Spain	Malaysia Philippines
	Low	Japan		Taiwan South Korea

Fig. 5.1 Scheme for assessing market potential

If you draw out a grid as illustrated in Fig. 5.1, you can begin to slot the markets into the boxes formed by the intersections of the vertical and horizontal lines, as the example shows. So, if Holland and Belgium come out highest in your analysis (as in the example) then they are your two highest priority markets in terms of potential and accessibility, and so on. In the example South Korea would come bottom of your priority list, given its low potential and low accessibility.

The next stage would then be to go into a much more detailed market mapping exercise, which you will need to do in order to create your marketing plan. The list below outlines all the information you will need to find to begin to build up a picture of the market. If it looks formidable, help is at hand. You can find most of the information you need from the sources listed below. You will, however, have to do some estimates to work out your market sizes and sooner or later you will need to make some exploratory visits to the markets you have selected. However, let's take one thing at a time.

Research methodology

If you have not been trained in market research, or have no experience of it, what we have described will no doubt be somewhat daunting. Basic research is not difficult, especially where there is a ready supply of published information. The method I recommend is as follows:

- Set an objective for the research exercise.
- List out the information you require.
- Make a plan for collecting the data.
- Collect the data and analyse them.

What we do in our business is to store all the information we collect onto a personal computer database; dBIII is perfect for the job.

Finding information

Many books make the recommendation to seek primary statistical data from sources such as ministry reports, central bank information, agricultural production information, OECD, EC and so on. In most cases this is unnecessary. Three-fifths of the information you require has already been analysed and published.

The list below should give you what you need.

Economic information

- Bank's *economic country reports* – National Westminster and Abecor Group (Barclays in the UK).
- *The Economist* – publishes periodical surveys.
- *Economist* Intelligence Unit – publishes economic data and commentary on nearly every country in the world.
- World of Information – publishes reports on the main trading regions with a limited directory.
- *The Financial Times* – produces country surveys regularly.
- Embassies – supply information (mostly on request) on doing business in their countries.
- *European Business* – produces a set of useful charts covering wages, office rents, comparable prices for the EEC in every issue.
- *Euromonitor* – produces an annual compilation of retailing for Europe. This is also available as an on-line database through Profile.
- Trade papers – carry considerable information about what is going on in the trade in the UK and target markets.
- The DTI – provides a vast range of information services (see page 53).
- Chambers of Commerce (particularly London and Birmingham) – Have a wealth of information (see page 57).
- SME Task Force (DG23) (see page 55).

All this information is ready and waiting to be examined. You can buy any piece for a relatively low outlay or you can find them in public libraries, university and business school libraries, the Institute of Directors in Pall Mall and the DTI's Statistics Intelligence Library to mention just a few. Profile has a number of on-line databases easily accessible through your PC.

Assessing market size

The information sources listed above will give you most of the information you require but you will be lucky to find precise market details for your product. You may, however, obtain enough information to go on to make some rough calculations against which to carry out more precise research later.

There are two methods for assessing market size where you cannot find precise information. The first method allows you to make an approximation of the existing market. The second helps you calculate the potential market.

Assessing existing market size

First calculate the domestic capacity of the target from:

- company reports, stockbroker reports, credit status reports;
- government production statistics;
- packaging suppliers;
- production machinery statistics (if these have to be imported you are likely to find these from customs statistics).

The aim of this part of the exercise is to work out the maximum level of production capacity for products which interest you as direct competitors.

The next stage is to analyse the imports by the target market for relevant product classifications.– again, customs statistics will provide you with the information you need.

Next analyse the exports of the relevant product classifications made by the target country.

These three pieces of information will provide you with important clues as to the size of the market. It will be your conclusions from the arithmetic and your judgemental interpretation of the information which will give you a guide to market size as follows:

- Domestic production capacity plus imports less exports will give you a ceiling to the existing market size.
- Now look more carefully at the information, e.g. high imports may suggest there is a large domestic consumption not met by local production, so local production capacity (less exports) is fully utilized. Low exports may help verify this assumption.
- High exports will indicate either that there is a ceiling to market demand or that the exporters have considerable competitive advantages.
- Now look at relative prices. If they are high this could indicate that the market is growing; if they are low the market would appear to be saturated.

So what have we produced to aid us in the calculation?

- We know the market capacity in volume terms (including imports).
- The rate of imports and exports will help us determine the level to which the market demand is met in volume terms by local manufacturers.
- Prices tell us the state of the market.

All we need to do is multiply whatever volume figure we come up with by an average market price to put us somewhere towards estimating the existing market value.

Assessing potential demand

The way to assess potential demand is to find some factor which you can estimate accurately and which can be used as a basis for an estimate. Say, for example, you wanted to calculate the potential for window fasteners in a market: you could calculate a potential based on house-building statistics. Another common method used to determine consumption potential is to assume the proportion of income that is spent on a particular market for a product or service. To do this you have to take the national income figure published by a government and relate this to demographic and social information, i.e.:

- the total population,
- an analysis of the proportion of the population falling into income groups,
- wage scales,
- family size,
- relative prices,
- retail sales statistics,
- health statistics,
- spread and level of education.

You can then get a fix on potential by making a comparative analysis on another market for which you have information, i.e. if in the UK the market size for widgets is £20m p.a., how does the market under study compare in social and demographic terms with the market you know? What information can be drawn by making comparisons? Obviously such a study would rule out a wide range of products where culture, climate and geography make markets unreliable for comparative purposes. It would be statistically difficult to compare, say, Malaysia with the UK, but you could compare Malaysia with Indonesia.

Comparative analysis only becomes feasible if you can find similar markets. As you collect more and more relevant information on markets you can, of course, begin to form them into clusters for analytical purposes.

Commissioned research

If you need professional support in your research there are three approaches you can make.

- The DTI's Market Research Scheme will provide professional advice in setting up a research project.
- There are several hundred qualified marketing consultants registered to carry out the DTI's export and marketing initiative projects. Fees tend to range between £350 and £450 per day. Many market information reports will take less than three weeks' work. Grants are available to cover a portion of these costs. A registered consultant can probably work out the whole project and costs for you and help you make your application for a grant.
- More expensively, you can employ a market research organisation to carry out detailed work. At an advanced stage, commissioned field research will probably be necessary. The initial investment may not only save you costs of initial mistakes. It will help you find the information you need to match more closely your market opportunities with the right strategy and resources.

Commissioned customer research

Customer research involves studies of buyer behaviour, attitudes, preferences and tastes.

It is used to test products, distribution strategies and advertising, and to find opinions and preferences, for a whole range of buyer goods and those who influence them. It uses scientific methods of data collection and analysis. Most customer research needs to be handled by professional marketing research organizations. The principle of customer research is that it uses samples or groups of respondents. Very often psychologists are needed to help collect and interpret data.

There are basically two approaches to the process:

- sampling a large universe of respondents through carefully selected or random samples of targeted respondents;
- using groups to study their behaviour and/or the responses that are generated through group discussions.

The former method produces statistical information that can be scaled up to be representative of the larger universe of the population sampled.

The latter is used to test reactions, perceptions and preferences. The results can be expected to be fairly representative of the larger population but are not statistically accurate. They do, however, provide a good guide for decision making in such areas as new products, packaging appeal, new flavours, colours, advertising and so on.

Customer research is a useful means of getting information about customer needs, aspirations and values. It helps identify their habits and loyalties. It uncovers information it is not possible to obtain by broader information gathering from published material. It also helps determine the implications of those difficult areas such as culture and custom on product acceptability.

Commissioning customer research

For most products, particularly consumer products, customer research is difficult to carry out using in-house resources where neither the skills nor the people exist. It is, therefore, necessary to call in a marketing research organisation.

You can divide the commissioning process into three stages, namely:

- Finding and choosing the right organisation for the project.
- Briefing the chosen organisation.
- Receiving the final report.

Choosing the right organisation

The selection process offers you three types of organisation:

- A UK marketing research company who will subcontract the work to an organisation located in the target market.
- A marketing research company situated in the target market whom you will have to brief yourself.
- A multinational research company which has a branch or an associate company in your target market.

UK marketing research company

The advantages of briefing a UK company to subcontract the work is that you can clearly brief the project in the UK and then let a professional organisation set up an overseas subcontractor to get on with the job. The disadvantages are that you will have little direct control over the project. It will be up to the company you appoint to select and direct its overseas collaborator. In assessing cost, make it clear that you are not paying for the UK company's lack of overseas offices and that the price quoted should carry no premium for this.

Local marketing research company

The advantages are that you make your own selection decision for the company which will execute your work based on your own perceptions of its attributes. The disadvantages are that you will have to travel and spend time in the selection process. You will have to spend time directing and coordinating activity.

Multinational research company

The advantages are that you select and brief the company's UK offices. They will then communicate the brief and direct the project on your behalf using their own people or associates. The disadvantages are usually cost. Multinational companies thrive on work from large companies and have voracious appetites for fees.

The brief

Your brief needs to be objective and specific. The key element is the objective. It is very easy to lose sight of the objective, so you need to revisit it at every stage of the project.

The next set of problems stems from translating the questionnaire. Questionnaires are difficult to phrase at the best of times. The translation process can lose the semantics of key questions. One way to check the questionnaire is to have a back-translation made from the foreign language to English by an independent translator.

The final report

Most market research companies like to present their final report and then leave copies. You will probably find it more beneficial to receive the documents and to have studied them before the presentation. This is especially useful if you have to visit the country where the research project was executed. It will give you a chance to study the report and formulate questions before the presentation meeting. It also saves you from the shock of going to a presentation where the results are far from what is expected.

Using the research

Given the tremendous amount of money spent on market research by industry, a considerable proportion of the research is either poorly interpreted or discarded. The smaller business is making a major investment when it undertakes market research and skills are needed in interpreting results. It is easy to interpret a highly positive report. It is less easy to interpret a piece which is inconclusive. The hardest to interpret is a highly negative report – fundamentally because it gives you few clues, except what the customer refuses to accept.

Interpretation of results needs care. If the report says 75 per cent of the sample like what you are offering, you have a high probability of success. If it says 5 per cent would buy your product, it does not mean a 5 per cent market share. It indicates that *nobody likes your product*!

Your marketing research provides you with a valuable insight into the market. It gives you information that nobody else knows. The problem for many companies is that they focus on the positive factors in their findings because they can use these in their sales presentations.

What you should focus on are the negative factors. The reason is simple. Give anybody ten reasons to buy something and it will be the one reason against which will spoil the sale. Look at your negatives closely and see what action can be brought to bear to eliminate them. By reducing negative factors you increase the probability that the success factors will work more strongly.

Every piece of research will indicate some positive responses but they are inevitably overstated against the negative issues. Ask first what your respondents disapprove of before you look at what they like. The message is not only to look for positives but test for negatives!

5

Government support for research

There are a number of research schemes for small businesses embarking upon or expanding their export business. They are prone to change but at present grants can be made for research carried out either on behalf of the company or by the company. However, you need to make your move quickly. The effect of competition rulings within the EC will remove most financial support for intra-community trade by the end of 1992 and will, before too long, begin to affect support for non-community trade.

DTI Statistics and Market Intelligence Library

The Statistics and Market Intelligence Library in central London is an Aladdin's cave of information. It has a microfilm database on products and markets, and a comprehensive collection of foreign statistics, trade directories, development plans and other published information.

The library is open Mondays to Fridays for personal users from 9.30 a.m. to 5.30 p.m. Very often short enquiries will be taken by telephone.

Export Market Research Schemes

The BOTB will offer you free advice on how best to set up a market research project. More importantly it will help with up to half the research project's cost, up to a maximum of £20 000. Again this subsidy will almost certainly be removed in the next few years to meet EC legal requirements. You can commission your study from independent consultants or execute the project yourself.

The rates and criteria vary and a degree of negotiation is probably necessary. The criteria expected by the DTI for all marketing research activity is that work be done objectively and to a high professional standard. Grants are available for:

- Marketing research done through an agency both for commercial projects and multi-study projects.
- Part of the overseas travel and subsistence costs for in-house desk research projects.

The DTI, however, holds the right to inspect finished reports before issuing payment.

The kind of things the DTI is often looking for in setting priorities for providing awards are:

- The experience of applicants in market research (first-time projects are encouraged).
- The share of the target market presently held by British firms.
- The level of expertise and qualifications of people or organisations assigned to the project.
- The objectives, methodology and costs of the research project.

List of services available through the DTI

- Lists of foreign commercial agents seeking British principals.
- Cooperation opportunities in fields of joint ventures, licensing and trade marks.
- Market reports by market.
- Short market pointers to new trade opportunities.
- Tariff and import regulations changes.
- Quarterly reports on the up-to-date economic and trading situation in more than 100 countries.
- International trade agreements.
- Calls for tender.
- Source of supply enquiries.
- Advance information on trade fairs, British weeks and store promotions taking place with Department of Trade and Industry assistance.
- Information on foreign buyers visiting Britain.
- Financial assistance for inward trade missions to the UK of delegations of foreign businessmen. These missions, however, must be collective and sponsored by a trade association.

- Market research assistance to British exporters through DTI Export Marketing Research Advisors.
- Help from the Group Export Representation Unit for groups of British companies to set up representatives or foreign operating units.
- Contributions from the Overseas Projects Group to the coordination of efforts of British companies with other UK organisations in either the private or public sectors.
- Assistance and guidance when British companies are affected by regulations imposed by other countries and international organisations.
- Information and assistance from the Overseas Publicity section in seeking the most effective ways of providing publicity for a UK company's products.
- A service provided by the Export Service Division or one of the regional offices of obtaining samples of foreign-made goods for testing by UK companies.
- Help with documentation through SITPRO.
- Information from the Central Office of Information regarding foreign communications media, and arrangement of visits to factories and companies for especially invited guests from abroad.
- An insurance service for British exporters provided by the Export Credit Guarantee Department, which also provides an information service (see page 142).

The services available from the BOTB are summarised below.

BOTB Services

Scheme	Average no. of projects 1984-7 (per year)
Export Market Research Scheme	915
Export Representative Service	369
Market Prospects Service	106
Overseas Status Report Service	1040

Source BOTB

EC Support for small to medium sized enterprises

The SME Task Force (DG23)

The Small and Medium Sized Enterprise Task Force was set up by the European Commission as part of its community enterprise policy.

Its aims are to encourage and assist in developing and creating new firms, helping small firms to grow and visibly providing enterprise. It is not in the business of protecting small businesses from competition within the European Community but of providing support and infrastructure to enable entrepreneurs to benefit from the enlarged European domestic market.

The SME Task Force, according to its Director, Alan Mayhew, has identified that small businesses in the EC need:

- Advice
- Information
- Help

Yet in setting out to provide support for small companies, its aim is to:

- Avoid creating new bureaucracies.
- Simplify regulations covering small businesses.
- Break down protective barriers to trade which have hitherto prevented healthy competition and starved businesses from access to each other's markets.

The SME Task Force, however, does not protect or subsidize smaller businesses. What it is doing is unique and of tremendous value to small firms.

By harnessing existing structures of Chambers of Commerce and consultancies, it is creating networks through which smaller businesses can gain information about such areas as community R&D projects, training, seed capital sources, and so forth.

At the same time it acts as a body through which suggestions about issues affecting smaller businesses can be fed to the European Commission. It also costs all the effects that new legislative proposals made by the Commission will have on business, thus offering a channel of communication for the smaller company to influence Community policy for trading both at home and in the wider European domestic market.

The BC Net

Through the creation of the BC Net in November 1988, the SME Task Force has created a network through which companies can develop cooperation strategies through:

- Finding new markets abroad.
- Finding partners in community countries.

At the time of writing the SME Task Force had about 40 centres operating in Europe. The target is 200, all of which will become active through existing institutional structures such as Chambers of Commerce and Export Centres.

Government/private network initiatives 'active exporting' programmes

A major new DTI initiative launched in January 1989, 'The Path to Active Exporting', is designed to fill a major gap in the ability of smaller companies to enter exporting.

The DTI recently commissioned a team of consultants to research the problems faced by potential exporters. The resultant report, *Into Active Exporting*, pinpointed expert guidance as one of the main needs. The report found that if passive and non-exporters undertook an export programme with the right help and guidance, not only would their businesses benefit from expansion but they would make a significant contribution to the UK's balance of payments. A nationwide Active Exporting programme, based on Chambers of Commerce and with DTI support, is the result.

The kinds of activities performed by Chambers of Commerce in *Active Exporting* are illustrated by the list of services offered by the London Chamber of Commerce, which covers the area bordered by the M25, in its 'Export Now' programme.

5

The Export Now Programme

London Chamber Export Now takes the form of individual action programming guidance provided by specially recruited Export Development Advisers backed by the Chamber's international trading expertise.

- The *Export Now* team give eligible companies a confidential and free export audit to assess each company's potential to undertake an active export programme.
- With a Green Light Audit, showing that both the company and the experts agree that an export programme is justified, we will produce a tailored management programme commencing with a First Stage Action checklist to cover initial market selection and first action steps into the market.

The coverage will include:

Markets	Payments
Credit insurance	Transport
Selling channels	Documentation
Customs requirements	Export office organization
Competition	Promotion
Trading term	Regulations

- First Stage Action will be prepared and agreed with companies in one-to-one counselling sessions with the London Chamber's Advisers. On top of their own experience, they have access to the London Chamber's specialist international trade services.
- To help the new exporter, the Adviser will agree a Second Stage Action counselling date with the company, to review progress and advise on follow-up export steps.

Reprinted by courtesy of the London Chamber of Commerce

The costs of entering the programme are minimal. The initial audit work is free and thereafter counselling is charged at a nominal rate of £15 per hour.

A new role for Chambers of Commerce

Unlike those of many of our continental neighbours, membership of Chambers of Commerce in the UK is not compulsory. Yet the role which Chambers of Commerce play in exporting is growing rapidly. Whilst services such as documentation, organising trade missions and joint-venture exhibiting have been in existence for years, their importance will evolve for exporters over the next year or two.

For the small, passive or new exporter Chambers such as London and Birmingham are opening important new ground for export support. This is coming from two directions.

1. They are providing infrastructural support for the activities of the SME Task Force with its networks such as BC Net.
2. They are acting as agencies taking on initiatives sponsored by the DTI – especially in the area of the *Active Exporting* programme.

Key Chambers (see Appendix 4) have therefore the unique ability to fuse both SME and DTI services to provide:

- Information,
- Services and
- Consultancy,

as well as acting as advisors to both the SME Task Force and the DTI to express the needs of their clients and members back to these sponsoring organizations.

Whilst membership is a prerequisite neither for the *Active Exporting* programme nor for access to the BC Net, membership of key UK Chambers such as London and Birmingham (and others listed in Appendix 4) will provide a basket of benefits which greatly surpass the costs of membership. For further information contact the Association of British Chambers of Commerce (see Appendix 4 for address).

5

6 Organising for export

Finance and resources □ Organisational options □ Agents □ Distributors □ Export houses □ Other methods of carrying out an international business

Two key questions we need to resolve are: 'How are we going to get our goods distributed in our export territories?' and 'How are we going to finance distribution and marketing costs?'

Finance and resources

The temptation to find importers and let them get on with it tends to lead to a series of *ad hoc* deals rather than gradually expanding new markets. The problem for most small businesses is finding the finance and resources to establish reasonable market positions.

Most available texts on the market provide little advice other than to suggest that the small business might use third-party importers or agents to sell the firm's products and then to make a host of suggestions on how to promote them 'on the cheap'. The flaw in the argument, as any business person will tell you, is that you cannot maintain a business which is marginal. Such a policy ignores both customers and competition. Whilst entry risks may be inexpensive and low, the costs of supporting such a business may not make it viable.

The small business, therefore, needs to approach the issue of finance and resources from a slightly different perspective from that of larger firm. The financing of distribution and marketing needs to be tackled as a single issue rather than two separate ones.

The three factors which will affect your approach to finding the right methods of organising for export are:

- The length of the channels of distribution.
- The level of service support your product requires.
- The level of promotional marketing support needed to enter and sustain market position.

Length of channels of distribution

Your product will pass through a number of stages before reaching the final user. It will have to cross a few hurdles before your consumers can find and purchase it.

Obviously, if you are exporting goods which are bought by industrial users, you will require a different sort of organisation to distribute your products than one selling consumer products which will have to pass through wholesalers and retailers to reach your final user.

Level of service support

If you are selling technical products to industrial end users, then you will need to organise around the level of technical support your products require. If they are fast-moving consumer products, you will need to take into consideration the need to merchandise your products at point of sale. Where your products involve service agreements, again you will need to take account of this in choosing your organisation.

Level of promotional marketing support

Do not think for one moment that you will not need to spend promotional monies on marketing your products in export markets. The need to create awareness, trial and purchase are just the same wherever you sell your products. If you are new to the market, the amount you will need to spend will be relatively high. Do not get taken in by the spurious advice on how to promote your products 'on the cheap', found in so many texts on small business exporting. If you have to promote your products in your home market, you will have to promote them in your export markets (see Chapter 9). The two factors you need to think about now are the focus of spending and the costs of entering the market.

If you are selling to industrial end users, your promotion will be centred around salesforce costs and promotion supporting its efforts. If you are selling consumer products your costs will be focused on advertising and PR to inform and motivate consumers to buy.

The cost of entering a market for the smaller business will be the major consideration in selecting options for organisation.

Organisational options

Your options will be governed by the three factors above.

You need to list out:

- The channels of distribution through which your products will pass to reach the end user.

- The levels of service support you require.
- The focus and cost of entry.

You then need to compare these with the advantages and disadvantages of the options listed below:

- Sell direct using your own resources.
- Enter a collaboration arrangement with a large manufacturer in a similar business.
- Form a joint marketing venture with a partner in the export market concerned.
- Use agents, distributors or export houses.

Use your own resources

Many small businesses sell direct to their channels of distribution or end users. This method is particularly applicable where:

- There is a limited number of customers.
- Service levels are minimal.
- Marketing costs are low.

Four examples serve to illustrate the point:

- A company sells tailor-made electronic components to a narrow range of customers. The intermediate components are imported into the UK and put together to match designs by half-a-dozen customers in Europe. The firm's expertise is in assembling components to meet an engineering specification at a low cost.

  The technically trained export manager visits his customers regularly to take design briefs and orders. The level of technical support is based centrally at the company's production facilities. The speed at which the company can respond to customer design specifications is its key competitive advantage. The firm's marketing activities are centred around exhibitions through which they attract new customers.
- The second example is a company which produces designer label garments, ceramics and luggage. Rather than rely on distributors and pay large sums in advertising, the company has aligned with a number of prestige departmental stores on an exclusive basis in a number of countries. The company's competitive advantages are the competitive quality of its products and its flair for design. Whilst the products maintain their own brand identity, the exclusive outlets through which they are sold take care of marketing and store promotion.

- The third example is a company selling Scottish smoked salmon. Again the company, through well organized trade missions, was able to sell a high-quality product direct to a limited number of key retailers under its own brand name. Again the quality of the retailer matched the quality of the product – meeting end user demand.
- The fourth example is a firm expanding into export markets and realizing that despite the level of potential demand the cost of market entry would be beyond its reach in terms of distribution and advertising spend. It decided therefore to offer the high-quality shirts it made as 'own label' brands to a number of large multiple retailers in various countries. Its costs of entry were low and it learned a considerable amount about its markets through this route. It has gradually been able to offer its own brands on the back of the own-label business.

Enter a collaboration arrangement with a major manufacturer in a similar field

For the small business this is an ideal method of expanding internationally and is particularly suited where:

- The exporter's products are innovative with large potential sales.
- Costs of distribution, marketing and service are high.
- The level of sophistication in marketing is high.

This arrangement is often termed 'joint marketing' or 'piggy back'.
There are four ways of approaching such an arrangement.

- Collaborate with a UK company with an international marketing organization
- Find collaborators in foreign markets.
- Form a mutual arrangement through which you sell your partner's products in the UK while your partner's firm sells yours in its own country and even its export markets.
- Enter a corporate venturing arrangement with a major company on the basis of equity investment.

Collaborate with a UK company

One of the features of even quite large international companies is that very often their export or international subsidiary company management organisations are divisionalized or in some way separated from their UK marketing divisions. Whilst many have a strong inventory for the UK, many are struggling to find products for their export or overseas subsidiary operations.

If your products are seen either to fit into their general export range or to plug gaps in the ranges sold through their subsidiary companies, an international firm might well be persuaded to take on your line.

You will need to do your homework very carefully to find the right people to whom you can make your proposition. You may also find that the organisation you are talking to is divided into global regions. Where one region can see an outlet for your product, another may not.

Do not simply address a letter to a company or its Managing Director, unless you know the contact, but find out who is responsible for which territories and approach them. Another way is to visit their subsidiary companies abroad and to try to get in that way. Often subsidiary companies are desperate for new products – especially where the firm's UK research and development is focused predominantly on the home market.

Certainly from our own experience both of running overseas subsidiary companies and later of controlling a group of them, we were reinforcing subsidiary company product ranges from third parties (often from quite small firms) from Sweden, Ireland, the USA and the UK in various parts of the world. In fact our own consultancy practice has introduced a number of small firms to larger ones in this respect.

Find collaborators in foreign markets

Again, as in the UK, firms are often short of new products. Many have gaps in their ranges or have under-invested in research and development. Many, too, will face the same problems for their export markets and subsidiary operations.

A joint marketing arrangement with a major firm, when successful, is a much superior method of organising abroad than using conventional distributors – but you have to have a product which fits their range.

The advantages over the conventional distributor arrangement are:

- Your product will be marketed as one in the company's range – rather than as part of a selection of imported products.
- Your products are only competing with the firm's own products for marketing and sales attention – and not with those from a host of other exporters.
- Your partner will undoubtedly contribute to marketing expenses.
- You are likely to have highly professional marketing and sales staff working on your product rather than those which typify the market trader mentality of distributors.

● Your product will be subject to budgets and disciplines of sales targets in the same way as the company's other products.

The downsides, if you can call them that, are that you will have to accept that your product will be sold under the business policies prevailing in the company. You will not be able to exert your management style over your importing partner – the reverse may be the case. You may also have to accept that the joint marketing partner will call the tune on marketing policy and decisions.

If you can accept these conditions and also expect a lower margin, then very often the long-term benefit is much greater than using a traditional importing distributor. Chemistry between the two parties and the matching of policies and business methods will pay a key part in such an arrangement.

Enter a mutual arrangement with a foreign company

Here you can expand on the idea of a joint marketing arrangement with a foreign firm, the idea being that you handle your partner's UK marketing while your partner takes care of yours.

So in effect you are collaborating to run each other's markets. The deal might then be extended to your partner handling your product in its export markets.

An alternative would be for both parties to form a joint venture company to cover export markets for both.

To achieve this sort of arrangement both companies' product ranges and types of customers have to fit. In other words, you both need to be in the same market. This no doubt could affect relations where your ranges overlap or new developments cause this to happen. By working closely, however, you might well agree mutual avenues for product development.

Enter into a corporate venturing arrangement

Increasingly, companies with a high-technology base are offering equity to major firms to invest in product development and manufacturing capability. These companies therefore acquire capital and managerial input and access to the larger company's international marketing networks.

Whilst this is a relatively new form of collaboration arrangement, it is one which is becoming increasingly viable. The criteria which large companies such as BOC and Pilkington set embrace firms with a technology bias and future profitable development. The marketing and export opportunity may not be the key motive for the corporate venturer who is looking for technology but it should be one of the criteria set by small companies prepared to enter such an arrangement.

There are a number of consultancies, merchant banks and business financiers involved in creating marriages between large and small companies. NEDO has recently produced a study of corporate venturing.

Use agents, distributors and export houses

Export houses, agents and distributors are the traditional channels through which exporting takes place. All are to varying degrees middlemen in the process. As we will see, they each have different things to offer the exporter.

For the smaller business they are an option, particularly if the options mentioned above are not available. But remember one thing – each, although operating differently, has a common motive in mind, and that is *to carry a range of saleable products* for which they will find customers but will not finance the marketing.

Agents

An agent is in the legal sense someone who can act on behalf of a principal. In the strictest legal terms they can commit their principals to contracts.

Agents act as intermediaries in the process of securing sales, either as representatives or submitting for government tenders. They are also involved in setting up licence agreements or local production and so on. They are remunerated through commission payments.

They neither carry stock nor take title to it nor do they usually take responsibility for credit risks – unless they are *del credere* agents. The latter will charge a higher commission to cover their own financial risks.

Other than acting as a selling organization, agents do little in the way of promotional marketing, other than to despatch catalogues or direct mail advertising.

Agents are particularly useful in dealing with government contracts. In the Middle East it is almost impossible to sell to governments without the support of an agent.

In theory agents can be used as a substitute for your sales staff, but remember that they will normally act for a number of principals and therefore your products will compete for their time.

The main disadvantages of using agents are:

● They work entirely to commission and their selection of customers and the methods they employ to sell your products may not be entirely right for the customer base you are attempting to build or the image you want to create – selection will therefore be a prime issue.

- They rarely involve themselves in promotional marketing.
- They will concentrate on product lines most profitable to them.
- In many countries contracts between agents and principals makes severance difficult.

Agents are particularly useful for sales-led products requiring little in the way of a distribution network and especially government contracts. However, you must be able to provide the necessary service response where this is necessary.

Agents are a poor option where you need a high level of distribution service, promotional support and customer service.

Distributors

Distributors, unlike agents, buy goods on their own account and take title to them.

The way distributors become successful is to create an inventory of products (usually around key products) which can be sold as a packaged assortment to individual customers.

Exporters use distributors more than any other method of distribution and an estimated 80 per cent of British export trade is handled through them.

The services distributors offer to exporters are:

- stock holding
- managing sales and distribution
- managing promotional support
- organizing service and post-sales care
- sales reporting
- sales forecasting and providing information about the market.

A first-class distributor can offer an exporter a number of advantages:

- Undertaking all the activities necessary to sell and distribute the exporter's products, leaving the exporter to pay for promotional costs only.
- Offering their intimate knowledge of the market to help the exporter form marketing strategies.
- Developing a working relationship with the exporter to build business to the mutual benefit of both parties.

6

- Carrying most of the risk for a product-launch failure – whilst the distributor will have to bear trade debtors, stock losses, overheads and possible redundancy costs, the exporter risks only the promotional spend. This advantage, however, tends to make distributors very cautious about accepting new lines.
- Looking after the exporter's sales staff during visits to the market.

However, the disadvantages of using distributors are:

- The exporter's product competes for time and attention. If it is a slow seller it will tend to be given low priority.
- As in the point above distributors are reluctant to take risks, often making it difficult to get them to take on new lines.
- Where a distributor builds a substantial business for an exporter he may become very concerned that he will lose it should the exporter decide to set up a subsidiary company.

Export houses

Export houses play important roles in export management. In the UK they account for about 15 per cent of exports. For companies new to exporting they can provide useful professional advice, export marketing, administration and financial services. Many also act as buying agents who account for a considerable amount of 'passive' exporting.

Whereas British export houses have not developed into the mammoth general trading companies which are a principal feature of Japanese exporting, or filled the global role for exports in the style of the North American export management companies (EMCs), they have become more specialised in terms of products, markets and services. In so doing they offer a range of services to exporters.

Export houses fulfil three types of relationship between manufacturer, importer and export house, according to H.W. Bailey, secretary to the British Export Houses Association, namely:

- They buy on their own account as principals (i.e. export merchants).
- They act as agent for the exporter (i.e. export agents and managers).
- They act as agents for the buyer (i.e. buying and confirming houses).

Export merchants

As export merchants, export houses buy from manufacturers and resell where they can find a profit. It is a simple buyer–seller transaction. You will be dealing with a customer residing in your domestic market. If you do business through an export merchant you are dealing with an intermediary channel in the distribution system that is selling your goods abroad.

Agents for sellers

In the normal course of your business as a manufacturer, you will call on the services of your bank manager, accountant and solicitor. Likewise, to avoid the pitfalls of selling overseas, many manufacturers have built up a profitable relationship with their export manager.

Export managers are paid by the supplier on the basis of an agreed formula (which may include a commission on sales), so that there should be no increase in the price of the goods to the buyer. The manufacturer usually remains throughout as principal in the transaction.

As H.W. Bailey explains:

'In effect, the manager acts as the manufacturer's export department. He will be responsible for promoting sales and will then book the necessary freight space and attend to the financial and clerical work involved in processing the sale. He will follow up delivery dates (or delays) and deal with the formalities in the importing country.

'Where required, he will operate using the manufacturer's own headed paper. In addition, some managers provide a financial facility, making prompt payment to the manufacturer and, where necessary, extending credit to the overseas buyer.'

Agents for buyers

In many export transactions, an export house acts on behalf of an overseas principal, assisting in locating suppliers or dealing with those nominated by the importer. Several American and other overseas department stores work in this way through buying offices established in London.

Frequently, these 'buying houses' offer a financial service and, indeed, for confirming houses this is their principal activity.

In a confirming transaction, there is a 'triangular relationship' between the importer, confirming house and exporter as follows. Again, H.W. Bailey explains:

'The importer and manufacturer enter into a contract for the supply of goods.

'The importer and confirming house have their own agency relationship. Under this, remuneration in the form of commission is paid by the importer, so that using a confirming house need not involve the manufacturer in any cost. The confirming house may also extend credit to the importer for up to 60, 90 or even 180 days.

'The exporting manufacturer and confirming house enter into a separate relationship. By this, the confirming house adds its own "confirmation" to the overseas customer's order and thereby guarantees that the order will be carried out by the purchaser – that the goods will be accepted for shipment – and, most importantly, that the seller will receive payment from the confirming house on shipment, without recourse.

'It is this "non-recourse finance" which is the fundamental strength of the confirmation system. Once the manfacturer has been paid, on shipment, by the confirming house, no one has recourse to him for compensation if the buyer does not pay, provided the goods and delivery time are in accordance with the contract.

'Many confirming houses also arrange shipment and insurance, ensure correct documentation, and generally progress and despatch orders.'

The value of export houses to the smaller business

Apart from the role export houses play in passive exporting, they can be extremely useful if you are just starting to export, for not only can you use their export management services, they will very often finance small business export start-ups when other financial institutions will not. Also they can often find lines of credit for key customers for markets where these are difficult to locate. This can be critical if your business is large and suddenly you find your customer cannot obtain foreign exchange. I still owe a debt of gratitude to Caffery Saunders of Northampton for finding a vital line of credit to supply medicine bottles critical to a company I was trying to turn around in Nigeria – when none of the international banks would confirm letters of credit.

H.W. Bailey sums up the benefits offered by export houses:

'Above all, merchants, confirming houses and frequently, export managers, will pay the manufacturer on shipment. The risk of non-payment because, for instance, the merchandise is less marketable than expected or the importing country has insufficient foreign exchange, is borne by the export house.

'Cash flow problems, export credit and foreign exchange worries need not cause sleepless nights.

'Some 30 per cent of UK exports are insured by ECGD, but the manufacturers concerned might bear in mind that for a buyer default ECGD will only provide 90 per cent cover on a short-term contract, payable some months after the claim has arisen and been verified. A confirming house pays in full on shipment.

'Regarding their product range, as a whole export houses are interested in all items, "from pins to power stations". As for their markets, the main criterion is probably whether or not the central bank will permit remittance of foreign exchange.

'Export houses are the key to profitable exporting and expanding overeas sales. They can be contacted via BEHA's Directory (£17), or by inserting a notice (£28.75 per entry, £11.50 for repeats), in the Association's six weekly *Export Enquiry Circular*, which is sent to all 200 members.'

Other methods of carrying out an international business

There are three other options for creating a marketing presence in foreign territories that we will briefly cover.

None is truly an export process but they are options for reaching foreign markets as alternatives to direct export. They are:

- Local production.
- Licence agreements.
- Franchising.
- Setting up a subsidiary.

Licence agreements

Under a licence agreement a firm grants the right to another to use any saleable know-how or goodwill such as a product's name, or to manufacture or part-manufacture a product using its patents. The licensee then pays the licensor a fee for the use of this licence.

Licensing is a useful alternative to exporting where:

- A firm has saleable know-how that is attractive enough for a potential licensee to be interested in it.
- The size and cost of market entry are beyond the smaller company (e.g. in the USA).
- Tariff or non-tariff barriers prevent entry into a market.

The dangers to watch, however, are:

- That you are not giving away your technology.

- That the licensee will not fully exploit your licence or not use it to prevent your potentially competitive product from entering the market.
- That the licensee is both financially capable and not restrained from remitting licence fees (watch developing countries and those with high overseas debts).
- That you have a way of auditing the licensee's use of the licence.

Franchising

Franchising is a novel way of entering a market. It is basically a form of licence arrangement but one in which the licensee (franchisee) provides a contribution to capital, financial and other resources as well as paying a licence fee. The franchisor, on the other hand, has to provide many of the key ingredients to attract franchisees and to ensure the success of the venture. These will usually include a marketing package, promotional activity arrangements and services as well as key ingredients to make the product.

The success of franchise operations rests with the ability of the franchisor to provide an attractive opportunity to firms willing to become franchisees. Marketing investment, control over marketing, and management of the franchise scheme are absolutely vital.

Franchising takes a particular type of entrepreneurial skill. Whilst this may be beyond the scope of this book, numerous companies have found partners more than willing to operate their markets on a franchise basis.

Setting up a subsidiary or branch office

By getting your organisation closer to the marketplace and controlling your own marketing and selling operations you enjoy the benefits that focusing activity on a market bring.

The step may not necessarily be a large one. Installing a local manager to oversee your distributors' operations might be the beginnings of setting up a new company to manage the market. Certainly the focus of attention and the commitment demonstrated will add fillip to the performance in the market. The attractiveness of taking over your distributor's share of the profit stream will no doubt be a major incentive but it should not initially be the primary one. For even though the revenue will help provide the running costs of a branch or subsidiary, the step must be taken on the basis of developing the market. You must have the potential to build on the existing market base. You will have to maintain your subsidiary's growth through a sustainable flow of new products – or allow your subsidiary to acquire or develop on its own.

Your new subsidiary will be a new business. It will need to generate sufficient market share to become competitive in cost and price. If its role is to replace an existing distributor or joint marketing partner, it has to do so from the point of view that it can:

- Bring as much to bear in terms of marketing, sales and distribution effectiveness as the organisation it replaces.
- Provide a better means to develop the market in the longer term.
- Exploit your firm's intentions to create a wider presence in the market from a sustainable source of new products or widening opportunities for existing ones.

Avoid the danger of embarking on setting up a new accountable part of your business and then starting to milk it dry before it has a chance to grow and evolve. Do not replace a flexible working and profitable method of organisation with one less capable of building your markets for the sake of a short-term gain.

6

7 Internal management for exporting

Is a separate export department necessary? □ Product orientation □ Geographic orientation □ Evolution of export management □ Start-up phase □ Phase 2 – territory development □ Phase 3 – internationalisation □ Management of the structure

The traditional approach to developing an export business has been to dedicate a department to it. The advantages are the obvious ones of focusing skills needed to plan, transact and administer the exporting function.

More and more progressive firms are adopting the concept of 'global think' as a business philosophy. This means looking at the world as the potential market – many times larger than the more domestic business. The opening of the European Single Market has no doubt begun to register the idea that firms need to organise to exploit opportunities and fight competition internationally. Also, important domestic customers may be expanding into wider markets and firms will need to arrange their organisation to meet their needs.

Synergies from pooling product development to produce more universally acceptable products, scale up production and exploit core technologies mean that, for many firms, strategies are evolving along product lines. It is at this point in the evolution of a business that it ceases to be domestically orientated and becomes an international marketing concern.

The structure of the company, then, will reflect management's attitudes, vision and aspirations for the future of the firm. Thus, the need for a separate export department will depend on the degree of specialisation needed to develop foreign business. There will be a requirement for managing markets and administration. The extent to which these can be accommodated in the organisation will have a bearing. More important, however, is the need for export development to be set firmly on track. It will require the commitment of company 'champions' to get behind it and make things happen!

There is then at least one transitory stage between domestic orientation and internationalisation which calls for some kind of a dedicated organisation to pioneer the export business. Your decisions will need to take into account strategy aspirations, by considering the question: Is the export business an appendage to the existing domestic business, or the core of future strategy?

There are a number of essential export functions which have to be managed, organised and coordinated. These are concerned with:

- Marketing/selling.
- Distributor management.
- Customer service
- Shipping/insurance.
- Administration/documentation.
- Foreign exchange and credit control.
- Legal affairs.

In developing your internal organisation structure for exporting you will need to take care of these functions.

You will also need to remember that your organisation must allow for:

- Accountability,
- Strategy planning,
- Decision making,
- Delegation,
- Control,
- Communications and
- Motivation.

Above all your organisation needs to match your strategies and plans and the activities you will undertake to achieve them.

However, in smaller businesses people are a scarce resource. It will often be necessary therefore to involve people in more than one function and it is likely that they will operate as both 'head chef and bottle-washer'.

This demands a high degree of flexibility, flair and the ability of people to take on a wide range of skills. It will call for much broader-set capabilities for individuals in the team than is often the case in larger firms.

There will be choices to be made about what functions should be carried out within an export department or within the general administrative and distribution management functions of the firm, and those which will be put out to service organisations. Yet it is vital that both the marketing and customer-care activities work hand in glove, so that customers can expect marketing support and at the same time be assured that they can expect a high degree of service.

Is a separate export department necessary?

Where you are starting from a domestic market base with little in the way of active exports, it will be important to find a 'champion' or 'champions' within your firm to pioneer and drive the export business forward.

This individual or group will need to be highly committed, motivated and supported at board level to drive projects through to create new markets.

The project team might be assigned on a temporary basis to make things happen or form the nucleus of future management teams to exploit and manage the new territories and markets.

Sooner or later you will have to decide on whether or not to set up a separate export department.

Traditionally firms have tended to set up a separate export department to handle overseas business. Yet, more and more, the wisdom of so doing is called into question and much debate within companies has been opened.

The principal advantages of having a separate export department are:

- There is a team dedicated to export development.
- Skills are concentrated to plan, transact and administer exports.
- There is a profit centre created which becomes accountable for business and profits.
- The nucleus of an international division is formed.

The disadvantages, however, need to be carefully weighed against apparent advantages.

- There is a tendency for the export department to become the poor relation in the organisational structure – particularly where a firm is highly oriented to its domestic market.
- The export department will tend to evolve its business strategy in isolation from what is happening in the domestic market.
- It is often difficult to recruit the calibre of people to export departments who might otherwise be available to the domestic business. (This is a fact of life in many industries.)
- Management and staff attitudes are focused along the lines of being either domestic or export, thus preventing your best people from adopting a truly international outlook for the business and developing their skills accordingly.
- There are few synergies achieved between domestic and export business developments and often little cross-fertilisation of ideas.

There are therefore distinct advantages and disadvantages, and decisions regarding options will thus be made on the basis of trade-offs. Yet at the start-up of an export business it is more than likely that existing staff will be called on to participate in setting it up.

Herein lies the opportunity to approach the problem from a slightly different perspective. It is an opportunity to endow your business with an international orientation from the outset. Go back to the question posed in Chapter 4. Will your strategy follow a product orientation or a geographic orientation?

Product orientation

Where your strategy will follow the product orientation route you will be seeking scale advantages in marketing similar products to similar customers around the world. Your management philosophy will be based on opportunities to evolve and adapt products from core technology and production.

Thus strategy decisions will be based on ensuring that your product development and market investment decisions will be based on matching these to market opportunities. A separate export department would thus be inappropriate where this strategy is adopted – although you will need to provide the necessary export functions for your product divisions.

Here you would need to examine the functional issues to provide the skills necessary to manage, transact and administer your foreign markets. The functions would be largely operational and could be accommodated within your overall organisational functional areas. Even people dedicated to sales and promotional activities for individual territories could be accommodated within your existing marketing structure, on the basis that they assume territorial or regional accountability within the overall organisation.

Geographic orientation

Geographic orientation seeks scale advantages through maximizing the development of products for individual markets. The issue here is focusing management on projects to build the business on a market-by-market basis. The logic here would be to set up a separate organisation to focus resources, product development and marketing investment on individual markets.

Where the firm has a geographic orientation the logic of setting up a separate export department is entirely appropriate.

Evolution of export management

Let us take the position of a firm which has no active exporting business. The structure of export management will evolve over time. In the general order of events you might expect the firm to follow three phases.

- Start-up
- Territory Development
- Internationalisation

Exporting, as we pointed out, plays a significant role in each phase. It is important, therefore, to overlay your strategy development with a matching organisation structure, as shown in Fig. 7.1.

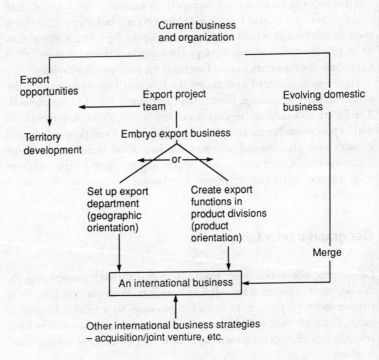

Fig. 7.1 Evolution of an international business

Start-up phase

At the start-up phase two vital functions are necessary:

- *A marketing function* to identify, plan and exploit initial opportunities in key territories.
- *A customer service and administration function* to coordinate the processes of ordering, documentation and customer care.

These functions are vital to planning and winning the business and for building a strong relationship with customers.

One of the common errors in setting up an export management is to ignore the importance of the relationship between the activities of marketing in building a business and those functions responsible for administrating it. An example illustrates the point.

- A small packaged-food manufacturer began selling in the Far East. As a result of a very professional approach by the firm's marketing manager, distributors were established and a marketing plan created. It was decided that the order processing, documentation and foreign exchange activities would be handled separately within the finance and administrative function. Problems began when distributors started sending in orders. Due to a breakdown in communications between marketing and administration (combined with the fact that the administration organisation was not 'up to speed' on exporting), customers began to get increasingly annoyed by the attitude, unhelpfulness and ignorance displayed at the administrative level.

  Leading trading companies in Hong Kong were astounded at the terms the firm was issuing for contracts. They were unable to trace the progress of orders. Time after time shipments were late, documentation was inaccurate leading to delays in payment, orders were then held up because of payment problems. Supplies became erratic, sales plans and advertising were delayed. The final outcome was that the project was only restored at the eleventh hour by board room pressure to solve the administration problem – even so, the finance director had proposed that the export business was more trouble than it was worth.

  The problem was solved by putting a person in the job of coordinating the processes between marketing and administration – to ensure that shipping was properly coordinated, and that documentation was correctly completed. Furthermore the administration department was debarred from writing letters or sending telexes to customers – all queries were channelled through the export administrator.

7

Phase one is about finding markets and customers and building a relationship between the firm and its new customers.

At this stage all other functions can be carried out either within the existing company structure or by using external organisations such as 'export managers' (see p. 68), forwarding agents, lawyers specializing in international business, banks, and so forth.

Phase 2 – territory development

As exports grow and new markets are entered, the primary consideration will be the management of marketing planning and selling activity. The recommendation is for you to begin to focus on resources required to manage markets. The ideal would be to put individuals with the right skills, experience and qualifications in charge of individual markets or clusters of markets (Fig. 7.2).

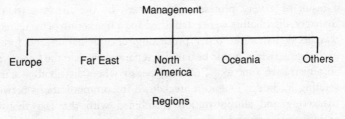

Fig. 7.2 Management of markets

The general principle is to:

- Develop areas of geography which have broad similarities in terms of language, culture and market structures.
- Create convenient business units for management and accountability purposes.
- Build markets based on opportunity priorities.
- Match market requirements with the right type of manager in terms of skills, languages and background.

There will obviously be some overlapping of responsibility with people taking on increasing numbers of regions.

The evolution of the team will no doubt follow the progress of market development. As each geographic region grows in terms of size and complexity more people will be brought in to manage and develop the business further.

This is where your management problems begin. For not only will you have more people on your payroll, you will now have to begin to coordinate your overall strategy in terms of products, markets and people.

You will need to set directions and goals to ensure that your marketing programmes are matched in terms of production, product development, finance, administration and qualified people.

It will be at this stage that you decide whether to create a separate export department or organise export functions under product divisions.

Phase 3 - internationalisation

This phase clearly goes beyond the scope of this book but it is important to touch briefly upon it. It is, after all, the outcome of international business development.

Exporting is, as we have already described, one of the activities involved in developing the international business. It will remain a part of the overall business even when the firm has emerged as a larger international company, at the point at which acquisition strategies and the evolution of large export markets permits the setting up of subsidiaries.

Exporting will play a part as:

- A shipping function between subsidiary companies.
- A marketing function to territories which are not occupied by the firm's own organisation.

The level of sophistication in terms of managing international finance, corporate development, and research and development will demand high-calibre people to manage line and staff functions. Yet in shaping your export strategy, at the outset some vision of its ultimate outcome will no doubt help you in both making the right decisions and providing a level of motivation.

Management of the structure

Successful management depends on six factors, namely:

- Vision
- Direction
- Motivation
- Accountability
- Synergy
- Skills

The criteria for a management structure are:

- Division of the structure into highly accountable units.
- Adequate means of communication between internal functions and external parties involved in the business.
- Allowing major decisions to be made quickly and easily but based on a disciplined framework to exact a clear rationale so that outcomes follow the general direction of the company's strategy.
- Encouragement of delegation within the management framework to reinforce accountability and to prevent autocracy from holding back business development.
- Creation and cultivation of a motivational environment which encourages creativity and commitment.
- Constant development and testing of management staff in terms of increasing skills, learning from experience and building ideas.
- Emphasis on project development to create new opportunities along planned lines.

8 Pricing for export

One-off deals and tenders □ Pricing for market building □ Pricing for market share □ Price differences between markets

There is probably no greater an area of complexity in carrying out international business than that introduced by the issues surrounding export pricing. Yet despite the myriad theories and anecdotes found in many exporting texts today, few tackle the pricing question from a marketing point of view.

Price is the value that potential buyers will put on a product when making a purchasing decision. Most buyers have an upper price limit in mind. This is conditioned by prevailing prices in a market and influenced by the attributes a product offers in relation to the buyer's need and the offerings of the competition.

Pricing is, therefore, a key element of the marketing mix and so it should be treated as such in marketing plans. The problem for the internationally orientated business is that it is extremely difficult to achieve or sustain an export pricing policy where:

- Prices vary from market to market.
- Channels of distribution margins vary from market to market.
- Differing levels of tariffs, duty and VAT affect end prices (especially where these discriminate against imported products).
- Foreign exchange fluctuations interfere with costs and margins.
- Parallel traders and international customers are quick to spot markets where prices are lowest and are likely to buy in these and sell where market prices are highest.

To set an export pricing policy, therefore, you need to go back to basics in terms of your marketing objectives. You need to treat pricing from the point of view of how it will influence your market building goals and how it will influence your profits.

The traditional view of price setting involves determining a minimum acceptable margin after costs. Yet such an approach ignores market forces and, what is more, assumes that a firm's cost base is similar to those of the competition. It is often assumed that where competitors pitch for lower prices, they are accepting lower margins; this is not always the case, for very often firms which focus on the market price will be looking at ways in which to bring costs in line with what the market will pay for their products.

The issues then are:

- What prices can you obtain for your product?
- What factors will influence your ability to earn a profit from the prices you set?

To tackle these two possibly conflicting issues, you need to determine the maximum prices you can obtain for your products at a level of market share which will make your costs competitive. In simple terms: What is the minimum market share you need to achieve to become competitive in cost and price? – and not What is the price you have to sell at to cover costs?

To adopt this approach you need to have a good knowledge of your own costs and the way they behave in relation to volume changes.

If you are to make a profit in the export market, then you need to understand your own costs and the expectations of your potential customers.

Another area of confusion arises where the issues surrounding 'one-off deals' and tenders are treated with the same arguments as those dealing with market building strategies. Let us, therefore, separate the two issues.

One-off deals and tenders

Winning an important order or a tender can have a major impact on the short-term business. Some orders may be large enough to keep production tied up for some time. Most one-off deals and tenders are won on two criteria:

- Price.
- Competence to deliver.

Thus any tender you apply for has to be based on the maximum price you can obtain and the minimum price which will make it a worthwhile proposition. Considerable care will thus be necessary in:

- Calculating your costs.
- Determining a competitive price.
- Financing the project.

Costs

The three areas of cost to consider are:

- Cost of producing the goods.
- Shipping/documentation/insurance costs.
- Credit costs.

The cost of producing the goods to meet the order need to be treated on the basis:

- The cost benefits achieved for the business by meeting the order.
- Less any special costs involved in meeting specifications.

The two elements of cost should be treated as discrete from normal production runs, i.e.

- As additional production, there is no need to charge your overhead costs where these are already absorbed by normal production activities.
- Extra costs incurred, such as conforming to specifications, overtime and so forth, need to be taken into consideration.
- Where production of the tender eats into the production output required for normal business, the costs of overheads which are not recovered because of normal volume shortfalls need to be added back to the costs of meeting the tender.

The problem with costing marginal production is determining what proportion of the actual production process is in fact marginal. It is often the case that, whilst in the central processes of production additional work is actually beneficial to overall cost recovery, it may create 'log jams' in later stages of production thus mitigating the full benefit.

Shipping/documentation/insurance

These are direct costs of meeting the tender and obviously need to be included in the overall cost.

Costs of credit

The time lag between the time you assemble materials for production and the time you receive payment ties up money. As you well know there is a cost attached, especially if you have high borrowings. You need, therefore, to add to your costs the cost of funds tied up in the project. To work out the cost you only need to know the prevailing rates of interest and the time which will pass before you receive payment.

Thus if you are tying up £20 000 for six months at an interest rate of 15 per cent per annum the cost is £1 500, which needs to be added to cost.

Deciding on the price

Once you know your costs, it is then a matter of weighing these against the value of the potential business. Your decision to pursue the tender will be based on the contribution it will make to sales and profits. The bottom limit to your quotation will be total costs plus costs of credit; the upper limit will be the highest price at which your quotation still remains competitive. For one-off deals and tenders, there is little sense in quoting to win the order if you cannot make a profit.

Thus when you quote you should face only one risk – of getting or not getting the business – and not those risks associated with the consequences of a loss on the deal. If you have a good knowledge of the industry and your competitors, there is a fair chance that you will be able to make a reasonable guess at competitors' tenders. Any firm winning the order on a loss-making basis is either making a financial mistake or is the beneficiary of aid or subsidies. (If such is the case in the EC, you may have grounds to complain to the European Commission, who will not ignore substantiated complaints.)

Of course, other factors, including exchange rates, will affect your competitiveness but if other things are equal and you persistently lose tenders on the basis of your quotations, two factors emerge which need remedying:

- Your costs are too high for the business you are in, and/or
- Your margins are set too ambitiously.

Pricing for market building

Pricing decisions for market building are based on a whole set of different criteria from one-off deals. You are concerned here in setting prices to achieve a level of market share which makes you competitive in cost terms. In this case price is one of the elements of your marketing mix and needs to be treated as such.

There are two options:

- Skimming.
- Pricing for market share development.

Skimming

This term describes an export pricing policy which suggests that you price more highly in export markets than at home. The aim of 'skimming' is to aim for a relatively low market share in foreign markets at high prices. The effect, in theory, is to gain additional profits from your production resources through higher margins. When you sum production over several markets (each with high margins and relatively low share), you make a significant difference to profitability when compared with the same levels of output devoted to the home market. It is, therefore, an attractive proposition for smaller firms.

It is, however, important to point out the drawbacks to such a policy, namely:

- If your pricing policy permits only a marginal market share, then your business will be extremely vulnerable – particularly if major customers refuse to stock the product. It will also be difficult to generate sufficient business to support your product in terms of promotion and service, both essential ingredients for selling at a high price.
- Small volumes of relatively high priced products may so inconvenience your production lines that increased costs mitigate the benefits of the additional margins.
- If you are successful then there is every chance that parallel traders will buy up your products where they are cheapest and sell them to your highly priced export markets – thus undermining your strategy.

If you adopt skimming pricing policies you need to take into full consideration their true economics in terms of the trade-off of volume and margins. You need to weigh the propensity for your strategy to be undermined by both the parallel trading fraternity and the lack of interest on behalf of stockists with regard to low-market-share products.

Remember too that a high-price policy needs to be supported by a high-quality product backed by adequate service to keep the loyalty of your customers.

Pricing for market share

For this strategy, price will be a key element of your marketing mix. There are two ways to approach this strategy, namely:

- Price well below the market average and then gradually increase price as you gain share.
- Price within the limits of prevailing prices and invest heavily in promotion services, etc.

Pricing for market share involves thinking and planning long-term. It is a favourite ploy of Japanese and Korean strategists and is used to great success. Yet it has to be understood that pricing for market share is a strategy based on maximising the advantages of production scale.

It is vital, therefore, if you are going to follow this strategy that you base your business plan on increasing production. The outcome of the strategy must be to reduce unit production costs to enable profits to be earned. Your strategy, therefore, has to be based on predetermining the capacity you need to meet demand and forecast unit costs at your targeted market share levels.

Whichever strategy you adopt, you must set your targets and marketing investment accordingly.

Your marketing plans must reflect your strategy goals in terms of market share and the value you will gain from it in terms of the prices people will pay and the volume they buy. You will achieve little if your plan aims for a high market share and your prices reflect aspirations for a lower level of penetration. Go for one strategy or the other – and plan your resources accordingly.

Price differences between markets

It is a fact of life that there are few products which do not show quite large differences in price between markets. Take razor blades; there is a 40 per cent price difference between the lowest and highest prices in Europe, for example.

The problem for products which have significant price differences between territories is that it encourages parallel traders and major customers to shop around for the cheapest sources of products. This can have a major effect on your domestic market prices. For example, one pharmaceutical company in the UK loses over 20 per cent of its sales to parallel traders from Belgium. The reason is that its prices in Belgium are 30 per cent lower than in the UK. This is due entirely to price control by the Belgian authorities.

Whilst it is easy to say you should avoid major price differences between markets, it is a much harder proposition to prevent them occurring.

Factors influencing pricing differentials

The key factors affecting price differentials are:

- Prevailing market prices – market prices have different norms in different countries.

- Exchange rate fluctuations between markets making it profitable for, say, a Belgian company to sell to a German one because of exchange rate advantages.
- Duty and VAT.
- The pricing policy of the supplier.

Achieving uniform prices is neither practical nor desirable. You need to watch very carefully those markets which have exceptionally high prices and those whose prices are very much lower than the average, for they will encourage merchants to buy your products where they are cheapest and sell them where they are most expensive: this has the effect of levelling prices downwards.

8

9 Export promotion

Promotional tools □ The phases of export development □ Start-up phase □ Market building campaigns □ Influence of early users on the market □ Checklist □ Maintaining your market □ Standardise or no? □ Control centrally or in the market? □ International client agency alignment □ How advertising agencies and PR companies organise to match international client needs □ Differences between markets □ The question of cost □ Step-by-step or all-out attack □ Paying for promotion

One of the greatest myths about exporting is that you need to put less into your promotional marketing effort abroad than at home. Just because there are myriad ways in which a certain amount of publicity can be achieved at low cost, it does not mean that promotional marketing should not be a central feature of your marketing plan.

A very great number of exporting texts tend to focus on what publicity you can get for nothing, rather than on the common sense of setting realistic promotional objectives – and matching these with activities.

Marketing promotion is an essential element in the marketing mix. To attempt to enter a new market without having thought through your promotinal communications ignores both customers and competition. Unless your customers are aware of your products they are not likely to seek them out. If your competitors bring more to bear to the market in terms of promotion, your voice will be drowned out.

If your success at home depends on promotional support, then it will need it in your export markets. Again return to the idea that you need to set objectives to succeed. Activity objectives have to be based on what has to be achieved and not on what you might get away with.

Promotional tools

There are four basic promotional tools, namely:

- Advertising
- Public relations (PR)
- Sales promotion
- Personal selling

Each has its own characteristics, strengths and limitations. A modern marketing company deploys each to meet specific communications objectives in creating a marketing-oriented dialogue with its market. Successful companies have long learned that through a well orchestrated mix of activities marketing plans can be economically and effectively achieved. They understand that the deployment of communications activities to be successful needs:

- Careful direction of messages to specific target audiences and target interest groups.
- Sustained competitive levels of activity.
- A means of measuring both the effectiveness of the messages it sends and their effectiveness in achieving objectives set for them.

In this context we can now briefly look at the role each promotional tool plays in the communications mix.

Advertising

The basic aims of advertising are to:

- Create awareness for a product or service.
- Promote key selling arguments.
- Add intangible quality to a product's image – thus reinforcing pricing.
- Remind buyers and users of the product or service and provide supporting information to reinforce selling activities.
- Create enquiries and leads for direct selling activities.
- Reinforce customer attitudes and foster reassurance.
- Reinforce company identity and corporate imagery.

Advertising strengths lie in using a highly targetable tool which can be aimed at fairly well defined audiences to dramatise a product or service.

Public relations (PR)

Public relations is used to help a business relate to its community, customers, employees and shareholders to help build and sustain goodwill. The fact that PR utilizes the columns of newspapers and magazines as well as non-advertising spots on TV and radio, makes the messages it transmits extremely effective for the following reasons:

- News emanating from the organisation reaches the reader or listener as media-originated reports – adding to its plausibility (it is not seen as advertising).
- Stories reach audiences who might otherwise avoid sales staff and advertising.
- Stories and events about the company or its products can, like advertising, be dramatised.

The important feature of PR-generated publicity is that the space it occupies is rarely paid for. Thus, whilst PR should be set specific missions in the promotional programme (e.g. creating a receptive and favourable buyer environment, providing knowledge amongst opinion formers and specifiers, and creating confidence amongst financial institutions and shareholders), it can be usefully employed to reinforce promotioned communications or plug gaps left by other promotional tools. It should not, however, be used as a substitute for advertising sales promotion or selling, for two reasons:

- It is difficult to sustain enough PR coverage on its own to achieve sufficient promotional impact on a market to have a significant effect on business development.
- PR rarely has the means of closing sales. Though its main strengths lie in creating awareness, generating interest and opinion forming, it cannot finely develop a sales argument without being heavily censored by journalists and editors.

Whilst many commentators applaud the virtues of PR as free or cheap publicity (particularly in exporting), to use it as a substitute for advertising is a gross mistake and a misunderstanding of PR's key strengths.

Sales promotion

Sales promotion involves all those activities and events which companies employ to excite customers and distribution-channel buyers into making purchasing decisions (other then advertising and personal selling). Through providing theatre and additional reasons to buy, sales promotion in short bursts of activity is used to:

- Reinforce reasons for trial during the introductory phases of a product's life.
- Reinforce product demand amongst customers.
- Provide tactical responses to competitor activity in market maintenance phases of a product's life.

- Win a higher proportion of salesforce time in multi-product marketing organisations, particularly where third-party distributor salesforces are involved.
- Reinforce product and company awareness.

The aim of sales promotion is to focus activity on specific marketing objectives. Sales promotions tend to be short-term in nature but are an intrinsic part of the overall marketing plan. Sales promotion should both support and be supported by other promotional tools (advertising, PR and personal selling).

Personal selling

Personal face-to-face selling provides a vital and intrinsic communications tool to the marketing mix. Because it is personal, it permits social relationships to build up between customer and supplier. It is flexible and alive, allowing the sales person to probe and test the selling proposal before closing the deal with the customer. It allows for past mistakes and customer dissatisfaction to be brought out and handled during sales interviews.

Personal selling plays a vital part in export development. The reason is that your business will be largely built on relationships fostered between your firm and your customers. It will be your own or your people's ability to close initial sales which will determine whether you build up a customer base or not.

Personal selling will also be a critical aspect of your marketing communications where your distributors or agents play an important role in securing sales for you in their respective markets. Their success will be determined by their ability to:

- Target customers.
- Reach target customers.
- Successfully carry out transactions with targeted customers.

As this aspect of promotional management involves both the choice and the management of the right third-party intermediaries, it is covered extensively in Chapter 13.

The phases of export development

Your marketing communications objectives will change as your export markets develop. Typically you will:

- Need to recruit contacts during your start-up phase.
- Plan market building campaigns during the territory development phase.
- Organise and coordinate your promotional marketing with other elements of the marketing mix once your business has taken off in each territory.

Start-up phase

The start-up phase will probably involve identifying potential customers and targeting them with marketing communications. Your primary objective will be to find the right partners to work with (see Chapter 6) and establish initial awareness amongst potential customers.

Your promotional plans, therefore, will involve activities aimed at creating leads and prospective customers. It will be about letting the market know you are in business and that you have something special to offer.

Your communication strategy at this stage will thus involve activities designed to support a selling role, i.e. those activities that will get you in front of 'qualified' prospective buyers or import partners.

Some of the activities you might consider are:

Advertising
- Advertise in trade journals.
- Employ direct mail advertising to prospective customers.
- Get your products listed in the various contact sheets sent out by Chambers of Commerce and Trade Associations.

Public relations
- Send news stories, product information and photographs to foreign trade journals (note that in the USA, you may have to pay for space).
- Get your news stories, product information and photographs distributed by the Central Office of Information (COI).
- Consider too opportunities for mentions on the BBC World Service new products announcements.

Promotion
- Participate in BOTB-sponsored exhibitions (see Department of Trade and Industry supplements).
- Take part in British Weeks and store promotions.

Selling
- Join trade missions.
- Make exploratory pioneering trips to target territories.
- Follow up contacts made as a result of advertising, PR or promotion.

Market building campaigns

In the continuum of creating sales, every business needs to focus its principle activities on to its markets to achieve:

- *Awareness* – to create a general knowledge amongst potential customers about the company's products.
- *Interest* – to stimulate potential customers into seeking more information about products in which they are interested.
- *Evaluation* – to allow customers to compare and consider products in relation to their needs and competitor offerings.
- *Trial* – to permit customers to make low-risk trials by taking samples, testing the product or having it demonstrated.
- *Adoption* – to enable potential customers to decide to make full and regular use of a product.
- *Reinforcement* – to ensure adopters (customers) are encouraged to remain satisfied and loyal to the product and promote its diffusion amongst their peers.

9

The aim of promotional communications is to assist each customer's learning process of becoming a loyal and regular user. Yet each individual will go through the process at a different rate, and many will never become regular users or loyal customers. The factors which affect the speed of the adoption process will depend on how long it takes for individuals to become aware of a product idea and their propensity to try it. Even so, people vary in their willingness to try new products – some are prepared to try them as soon as they come out, others show different degrees of caution.

Influence of early users on the market

If they are entirely satisfied with the product or service they are using, many early users will encourage others to try it. This role of early adopters is empirically proven and is very important because:

- Positive comment will greatly speed up the diffusion of a product idea in the market.
- Negative comment from early users will often have the effect of slowing down the general acceptance of a product or service.

Thus promotional communications must involve fostering a climate of reassurance and reinforcing positive customer attitudes. Furthermore, the company will need to ensure that good customer service policies are maintained to reinforce the product and image expensively created through promotional marketing. Satisfied users are not only the ones most likely to make repeat purchases; they can also have a large influence on the general acceptance of a company's product by the market as a whole.

If you adopt this approach and can successfully convert early adopters, your success is all but guaranteed!

It is important, therefore, to monitor your progress. You will need to check:

1. That your activities have been successfully executed (i.e. that campaigns have actually run, that the activities were accomplished).
2. That the results you achieved from the campaigns were in line with the objectives you set.

It is important to remember that where campaigns are badly executed, the results achieved fall very much shorter than the degree of success achieved in the execution. In other words, a 50 per cent success in execution will achieve considerably less than a 50 per cent success in response. It is also a fact of life that a successful campaign costs about the same as an unsuccessful one. So, in planning your campaigns, make sure that:

- The messages you are communicating will achieve a positive response.
- Your execution is 100 per cent effective.
- The results of your campaign are measured on the basis of successful execution.

Your market building campaigns, therefore, need to be targeted at those groups which might be described as *early adopters*, who having once gained some conviction and commitment to your products, are likely to help in the diffusion of interest and adoption amongst groups who enter the market later, providing you obtain an active and positive response from them.

This means that you need to ensure you identify those positive

attributes inherent in your products which will impress the early majority
– and that your products meet their expectations in terms of:

- Function.
- Quality.
- Value.
- Service.

You will need to do a certain amount of market research to test for key
factors in both your product and promotional messages which will
influence the behaviour of early adopters, for if they ignore your offerings
or gain a negative impression, they will not help create a market for you.

The issue of promotion involves careful targeting of audiences and
selecting messages which will influence early buyers to adopt your product.
It involves determining success factors in this regard and planning
campaigns accordingly. If you ignore promotional requirements or simply
throw money at the market, you are unlikely to be successful. If you short-
cut the process and fail to research your market and target audiences
adequately, your success will be more from luck than judgment.

In summary, you might use the framework in Fig. 9.1 to plan your early
market development plans.

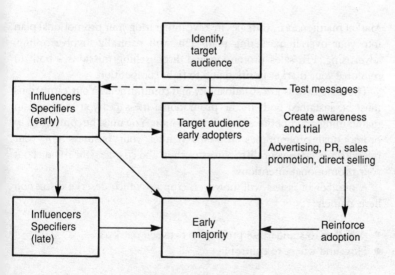

Fig. 9.1 Scheme for developing a promotional strategy

Checklist

1. Identify your target audience.
2. Test your promotional messages.
3. Identify influencers, specifiers, etc.
4. Test your promotional messages to influencers.
5. Create awareness and trial amongst early adopters through advertising, increase belief in your advertising using direct selling (as appropriate):
   (i) PR aimed at your target audience.
   (ii) Appeal to influencers through PR, advertising and direct selling.
6. Introduce promotion to reinforce trial and to secure repurchase behaviour.

Do not attempt to sell your product for functions which it is not best at performing and bear in mind that quality and value expectations are perceived relative to your competitors' offerings. A degree of market research to test for both product and promotional factors would be highly recommended.

Maintaining your market

Market maintenance strategies involve integrating your promotional plan into your overall marketing plan. This will naturally involve selling, advertising, PR, sales promotion and direct selling missions – both to reinforce your market position and to fight competition.

The watchwords are sustainability and commitment. Your campaigns must be sustained both in the promotional messages you send and in maintaining a competitive level of promotion. You must be committed to promotional programmes. It helps neither your business nor your relationships with your distributors to chop and change your mind about your promotional intentions.

A number of issues will, however, crop up which deserve discussion here, namely:

• Whether to standardise promotion between markets.
• How and where to control it.

These issues are closely related.

Standardise or no?

Once you begin to start selling the same products in different markets, there is a great temptation to use the same advertising material in each market. On the face of it, it makes sense to amortise the costs of materials across as many markets as possible.

There is little doubt that the international advertising budget represents a sizable proportion of marketing funds invested in the selling effort. Yet it is worth emphasising that the level of investment in an effective advertising programme can be little different from that spent on an ineffective one. According to James Killough, writing in *The Harvard Business Review*, more attempts to internationalise advertising fail than succeed, despite the experience, money, time and attention spent by large international advertisers.

Many companies are now beginning to question the whole basis for their rationale in producing standard campaigns. Greg Harris, in an article in *The International Journal of Advertising*, argues strongly against international standardisation of campaigns by questioning the arguments in favour of such an approach, viz.:

- Whereas it is quite possible to identify real economies in such areas as product standardisation, this is not the case from a policy of advertising integration.
- The media-led impact in increasing a global consumer homogeneity has been exaggerated. Evidence put forward to suggest that cultural and national differences are no longer profound is also not convincing.
- There is a much lower exposure to overseas advertising from travelling abroad. Exposure to international media is not yet of a scale that necessitates advertising integration.
- The fact that headquarters management possess marketing skills and talent not present in their overseas operations does not in itself assume that advertising integration is the right way to exploit or transfer skills.
- The administrative and political problems (not to mention the expedients required to circumvent local legal or media regulations created by advertising integration) are considerable and should be viewed as a distinct cost.

These arguments against global standardisation are powerful. The myths that creative and production savings can be made and that a global synergy can be achieved are difficult to justify. This is particularly true when the opportunity costs of missed sales are difficult to assess.

Control centrally or in the market?

The second issue is, who is going to control marketing expenditure? If you have not considered this issue, your distributors or foreign partners will have. The arguments in favour of central control are strong where exporting is the principal means of carrying out an international business, particularly if you do not have your own offices in a territory; they are:

- You control promotional activity in terms of message, media, timing and cost.
- You can instill your own quality critieria into production of advertising materials.
- You ensure that your campaigns *actually run* at the time you have agreed with your distributors or partners (because you make the decisions).
- There are opportunities to exploit regional advertising (e.g. cross-border overlays, satellite, international media, etc).

There are, however, some cirtical disadvantages which your distributors or partners will point out, namely:

- There may be difficulties in integrating promotional and selling activities where you are making the promotional decisions and your partners the sales decisions.
- Your partners may need flexibility and quick decisions to adapt or change campaigns.
- Local knowledge may have advantages in discussing and evaluating campaigns submitted by your advertising agency.
- Your partners may give the excuse that sales would have been better if they had been given a freer hand with planning the advertising.

The problem is that very many distributors think they know about advertising but are often limited both technically and in the way they approach promotional planning. yet their contribution is vital if they are to feel part of the planning of your business.

The ideal solution will be to involve your partners at the planning stages and ensure that materials which are produced meet your own quality criteria. As you develop your relationships with different distributors or partners, you will get to know to whom you can delegate and to whom you cannot.

It will also be necessary to decide whether you are going to use local or international advertising and PR agencies.

If you choose to use a local agency for your advertising and PR, the responsibility for coordinating activities and developing campaigns across a number of countries will fall entirely on your shoulders. Where you are selling different products to different markets, there is little to be gained (except possibly quality) from using other than local agencies. Where you are selling common products across a number of markets, you might consider the advantages of aligning with an international agency network to help coordinate activity.

If you choose the international alignment option, it is worth pointing out the different ways in which advertising and PR companies set up to provide an international network to meet client needs.

International client agency alignment

Some companies choose to align themselves internationally with a particular agency. There are benefits for the client, especially where there is considerable headquarters involvement in the international management of advertising.

The main advantages are:

- The head office client can talk directly to the agency head office.
- International standards can, to a certain extent, be imposed through the agency's disciplines in all the client's markets.
- The client has a certain amount of muscle with the agency because of the overall size of the account.
- The world advertising campaigns are coordinated to ensure overall policies relating to brand advertising are maintained.
- Global experience records of brand successes and failures can be maintained at the centre.
- International workshops of agency creative groups working on the same product in different markets become feasible.

The principal disadvantages are:

- There may be a tendency for over-management of the brand from the head office, to the detriment of local activities.
- An unnecessary over-standardisation of creative presentation may occur throughout the agency network, which stifles local contribution to advertising ideas.
- Although the global billing may put the client on the agency's head office list of accounts, it is frequently the case that at the local level the account is uneconomic and receives very modest attention by local agency management.

9

- The more countries in which a brand is handled by an agency network, the more probable that there will be conflicts with competing accounts, to the detriment of both client and agency.

Alignment provides a very useful way of coordinating advertising and PR internationally where:

- A product orientation strategy is central export development – thus requiring a degree of marketing harmonisation for international brands.
- Geographic orientation is in its early stages and advertising and PR are controlled centrally.
- The diffusion of corporate PR is an ingredient in the communications strategy.

However, alignment is not a particularly satisfactory option where export territories are well developed but where sales are made up by culture-bound products peculiar to their markets, because inputs from the agency's central office become irrelevant and lack the sensitivity needed for achieving local marketing objectives.

How advertising agencies and PR companies organise to match international client needs

Clients needing an international service will look towards agencies offering such a service. Some clients may themselves be in the process of expansion and require the services of an agency both to aid in their expansion by providing contacts and to survey and plan market entry by generally assisting missionary executives. Multinational agencies certainly have the edge in these circumstances. There are occasions where a smallish client begins to look abroad and seeks its agency's assistance. Where the agency itself has yet to set up in the client's target territories (it may itself lack foreign experience), it may actively look for ways of servicing its clients through setting up confederation agreements with foreign agencies or looking for compatible associates. The client, of course, may get the worst of both worlds when its own lack of experience is coupled to the inexperience of its agency.

James Benson of Ogilvy and Mather in London once quoted 'flexibility in matching clients' needs' as a key to servicing and gaining business from multinational clients. Flexibility in this sense means matching the client's needs. It also means keeping pace with the dynamic changes in environments where clients and media are contributors to a fast changing international marketing scene.

The following agency structures are the most commonly found.

Multinational agencies

Agencies which are really multinational enterprises in their own right, such as Ogilvy and Mather, FBC Publicis and McCann Erickson, are internationally established companies operating wholly or partly owned subsidiary branches in major world centres. To the multinational agency can be added the joint venture or partnership.

Confederations of agencies

A confederation of agencies describes a situation where two or more agencies work together to service common clients. In many cases the ties between agencies are often very close with strong coordinating managements which allow for a cross-fertilisation of ideas. There emerges a strong and effective client service. This gives the confederation the ability to mount and operate multinational advertising campaigns. In other cases, organisation and coordination are less effective and demand a high level of coordination by the client's own management.

Associate agencies

Some agencies use associates located in foreign centres to place business with local media on a shared commission basis. Such arrangements are very suitable for smaller agencies with relatively low-spending clients or where the level of business potential in a market is not high enough to justify investment in a branch. Most agencies using local associates as agents work on a reciprocal basis.

Centrally based one-office structure

Another method of operating internationally is by running a central agency which deals directly with media internationally. This is not as difficult as it seems, because in major centres such as New York and London there are central media representatives. These act as brokers for groups of publications, or they act for a major media conglomerate which owns journals, newspapers, radio, TV and cinema advertiser concessionaires. This method has a number of advantages in terms of control and obviously offers economies over previously discussed structural methods of international management. Distance may be a problem in that the centre may be remote from its markets, and executives are not in daily touch with their markets.

(Extract from *Choosing and Using an Advertising Agency*, Chapter 10, J W Dudley, Institute of Directors Publications, 1985.)

Differences between markets

The problems you will face in promoting your products in different markets will, of course, be influenced by cultural issues, legal issues and the differences of media availability and costs.

Cultural issues

Even where your products meet similar needs amongst similar market segments, the appeal of your advertising will be very much affected by cultural issues and buyer behaviour. This will influence your decisions on both the degree to which you standardise your advertising and the media you use.

It is important, therefore, to take very clear advice from your advertising and PR agencies as to the way you present your advertisements and PR, and the media you use. The argument should always return to your promotional objectives, of who your target audience is and how you reach them in terms of message and media. The rigorous and disciplined pursuit of identifying the match between message and media and your audiences is as important abroad as it is at home. The need for testing and monitoring becomes all the more important the less you know about a market.

Legal restrictions

Consumerists, politicians, the church and industrialists have, for varying reasons of public-mindedness and creating trade barriers, put pressure on national legislatures to control and police promotional activity. There is certainly considerable scope for tightening up doubtful areas of promotion and, whereas voluntary controls and codes have mitigated the need for punitive legislation, there are a host of regulations in each and every market with few common standards.

Legislation varies considerably from country to country and it would be necessary to fill several volumes if we were to go into country-by-country detail. Here we will go into the general areas of promotional activity covered by legislation and give examples where pertinent. By and large the law is used to control promotional activity in order to:

- Protect consumers from attacks on their credibility.
- Protect consumers from over-promotion of dangerous products.
- Protect special consumer groups such as children and the sick from activity directly aimed at them.
- Maintain free and fair competition.

- Avoid litigation through contravention of other areas of the law, e.g. betting and gaming legislation.
- Erect non-tariff barriers to trade.
- Defend language, religion and culture.
- Prevent sales tax avoidance (e.g. giving away taxed premiums with non-taxed products).

This list is as comprehensive as our researches allow; no doubt special regulations are also used to enforce political beliefs and doctrines. These are often discovered in censorship regulations which may be involved under the heading of defending language, religion and culture.

Laws which act as barriers to trade are subtly concealed in promotional legislation. In some countries time restrictions on market presence are imposed before importers are permitted to use TV advertising. This is a useful way of limiting marketing flexibility in planning a national launch by countries wishing to mitigate the influence of imports on the local economy.

Voluntary controls and codes of practice prevail in most advanced countries. These are designed to forestall legislation and to demonstrate, *inter alia*, a professional responsibility amongst communications and marketing industries. In lesser developed countries there are moves to set up voluntary codes through advertising and marketing associations as well as trade associations, careful to avoid unfair competition and the wrath of emerging consumerist organisations.

There is no doubt that in most markets the legal and voluntary controls on promotion present the international marketer with a host of unknown problems. The complexity of the international market in the area of promotional activity is a legal minefield for the unwary. In obtaining information on individual territorial legislation, you must seek legal advice in the markets concerned. Many bodies, such as the IPA in London, do produce booklets and information on marketing conditions in major markets. However, most minor markets, particularly lesser developed countries, are not so well covered. In preparing promotions, the use of local counsel is a must, both for interpreting legislation and on finding exceptions to it. The cost of poor intelligence in this area of international marketing can be as little as throwing away material and packaging, but in some cases it may incur litigation costs, fines and other penalties, or even the demand that a product be totally withdrawn. Furthermore, there is a mounting tide of opposition to some promotional practices, both within individual countries and from the international community. The criticism levelled at a number of companies, particularly in the medical fields operating in lesser developed countries, has emanated from opinion formers in the advanced Western countries.

Some examples of constraints in the EC are the limitation on the use of premiums in West Germany, the restrictions on the size of samples given out and the restrictions on the scope of sampling operations. In the last case, 100 per cent sampling is not allowed because this constitutes malpractice by temporarily squeezing out competition. In Belgium, lotteries and 'Mystery Man' promotions are banned, as is the selling of pharmaceuticals through promotion, advertising and point-of-sale material.

A bizarre example pertains in Holland: if you offer a self-liquidating premium at a reduced price, the article must have been on sale at the original price for three months beforehand. During the offer, the premium must be obtainable separately from the product and if anyone had bought the article at the original price before the promotion, they can claim 50 per cent of the difference from the price they paid!

There is a body of EC law being created which, together with new European broadcasting treaties, will at least begin to harmonise promotional legal issues. One word of warning, however, is that some of the regulations which apply in the UK will most probably be changed.

Media

Media availability differs from country to country. Firstly there are countries in which there is an ample selection of media to reach virtually any audience you define. This is particularly true in the EC, North America, much of the Far East and Australasia.

In developing countries you have the combined problems of limited media availability and lower literacy levels, which makes it difficult to reach consumer audiences through conventional means. Many companies marketing consumer products in lesser developed markets have used mobile cinemas and loudspeaker vans to reach large rural markets.

Secondly, the structures of media are different in nearly every country. In some countries TV and radio are readily available and relatively unrestricted, e.g. in the UK, North America, France, Italy, Japan and Hong Kong. Yet in others, magazines and press are more readily available, e.g. in Sweden, West Germany and Norway. The event of satellite TV in Europe may bring about change in this respect. Another surprise is the popularity of cinema in many countries as compared with the UK.

The reason for making mention of these examples is to ask you to approach each new market with an open and questioning mind about media availability. One client of mine had gone to extreme lengths to produce an advertising manual for his distributors. In it TV was stipulated as the primary medium for all advertising because it was live and dramatic and suited the product's positioning. The manual was rewritten after considerable face-saving when in eight out of ten selected territories TV was not the best choice of media because of lack of availability, restrictions and cost. The message is: do not pre-judge what is best for your products until the 'homework' is complete.

The question of cost

Launching into new markets involves costs, whether we like it or not. Each market entry has to be seen as a business plan and it is unlikely that you will go straight into profit. A large market demanding a high cost of promotional spend may take two or even three years to go into profit. This naturally puts a high cost burden on smaller firms. Yet we can find ways of reducing the impact of cost.

It depends very much on the type of product you are selling and the type of market and user to whom you are appealing. Obviously launching a consumer product will involve costly advertising compared with that of a business-to-business product.

To find ways of reducing the cost impact, three rules apply:

Assess what is absolutely necessary

Assess what promotional tools are absolutely vital to your market entry. A business-to-business product will probably mean a high level of direct selling with advertising to support the sales effort. Focus then on how many salespeople you will need, the cost of training, remunerating and motivating them, and what material samples are required. In this case the bulk of your costs must be focused on meeting as near as possible the minimum sales effort required to carry out your plans. Again using this example, you plan your promotional activity around salesforce support, finding the most cost-effective (not the least costly) way of supporting the sales activity, e.g. choose the right exhibitions and select trade press carefully.

The same thought process will follow for a consumer product where you will be focusing on the level of advertising expenditure you need and supporting it with sales and point-of-sale reports.

The maxim is spend as much as you need on the critical factors in your promotional mix and be mean with everything else. In other words, do not spread your costs over a wide range of activities, particularly those peripheral to the mainstream activity you have identified.

9

Set clear promotional missions

You can cut your costs of being effective considerably if you clearly define the missions each element of your promotional mix *has to* achieve – namely, sales prospects to be converted, audiences to be reached and opinions to be formed. If your success depends on converting a thousand industrial buyers, spend your money behind the sales attack, not on your distributors' favourite football team or the local mayor's charity!

Then, make sure that you put everything behind each mission to make sure it is properly planned and executed for, as we have said before, achieving half your objectives will achieve greatly less than half your results.

Get what you can for nothing

As we said at the beginning of this chapter, many books on exporting start off by explaining the huge array of services and options for obtaining free publicity. We have left this issue to the latter end of this chapter because free publicity does not usually generate a great deal of business on its own. Yet when you add it to your other activities, it can have a very significant effect.

Free promotion can be achieved in a number of ways; for example:

● Using government support, i.e. COI.
● Having free articles and news stories published in trade and consumer press or broadcast on TV and radio.
● Participation in conferences and seminars.
● Riding on the back of other people's promotions.

Yet the cheapest promotion you can get is word of mouth. It can account for up to 25 per cent of new adopters for some products, according to research done in the UK and USA. The criteria for making it work are exacting. There is a bare minimum level of awareness amongst your target audience above which word of mouth will begin to work given a percentage point or two, this level is about 35 per cent.

So how can you stimulate 'word of mouth' promotion?

● Reach specifiers and influencers with targeted direct selling, PR and advertising.
● Target your marketing investment to achieve a minimum level of awareness, say, 40 per cent.
● Drop sample the market (where this is permitted).

You will be paying for these activities in the short run but you will harvest the benefits later.

Above all, when you have spent time focusing your expenditure on critical promotional tools, set missions and extracted every ounce of unpaid-for advertising, remember it will be *your product and the service support you put behind it* which will make it a success. it will be the good words in the real free promotion of people's mouths which will bring in more users. How else do you think the Japanese are doing so well?

Step-by-step or all-out attack

The success of many small businesses at home is due to the gradual expansion process of building a market and the stealth through which they avoided confronting competition. If this process worked at home it is likely it will work abroad, particularly in large markets. The initial costs of entry are greatly reduced if it is possible to enter a region of a new market and gradually expand outwards. The benefits are also to be found in that you learn as you go.

The problems become difficult where there are national customers who cannot be brought into the business plan until you have reached a certain stage in your development. It might also be difficult to isolate local or regional media to bring adequate promotional activity to bear. As good fortune would have it, those large markets of North America, West Germany, France and Italy are among many where a region-by-region entry is highly feasible and, for many products, is the recommended method of entry.

Paying for promotion

There are three recommended ways of paying for promotion:

- Meet bills from your distributor and the media and pay them as they occur.
- Set your distributor an accrual account from which a percentage of the selling price is deducted to meet promotional costs (this is not a good method where duty is high because it brings down your CIF invoice price).
- Set a promotional budget from which a part is covered by accruals from local selling price and the balance is topped up by your firm.

Each has its own strengths and weaknesses but the last is probably the best in most cases. The reason is that it allows a certain proportion of the promotional budget to be raised locally from the sales effort and the amount necessary to meet your plans is under-pinned by your contribution. It can also be the most cost effective if managed well. The first method provides a bottomless pit if your distributor is not doing a good job. It is also the most expensive. The second limits promotion directly to sales which may mean that, if sales are slower than expected to start with, your promotional budget will be starved. As such it is not a good approach at the early stages of market development.

The third method has some clear advantages where the distributor's margin is adjusted at cost to pay for a promotional accrual.

The only danger to avoid in the recommended method is that your distributor will pocket the accrual as extra profits. You must, therefore, ensure against this possibility and adopt the first method if there is any likelihood of this happening.

10 Trade missions, exhibitions, conferences, British weeks and store promotions

Trade missions □ Planning your participation in a trade mission □ Finding out what missions are available □ Exhibitions □ Key criteria for a successful exhibition □ Major trade shows □ Lesser-known trade shows □ Research □ Set a realistic budget □ Design □ Transport and customs administration □ Joint venture schemes □ Shipping □ Protection of patents and trade marks □ Stand organisation □ BOTB services and exhibitions □ Conferences and seminars □ Store promotions □ British weeks

During your pioneering phase you will need to make contacts with potential customers, distributors or potential collaboration partners. This chapter is about some of the techniques you can employ.

Three very useful means of establishing contacts deserve some discussion, namely:

- Trade missions
- Exhibitions/conferences and seminars
- British weeks and store promotions

Trade missions

Inward and outward trade misions

Trade missions provide an attractive means of gaining information about markets and making contacts. Trade associations, Chambers of Commerce and other recognised bodies sponsor trade missions, usually with government assistance. They can play a very important part in export marketing for both the 'first-timer' and the regular exporter.

Inward missions are those organised to bring prospective customers, trade partners and specifiers to meet potential suppliers in their own countries. The sponsoring body organises presentations, contact events and factory visits, etc.

Outward missions are organised to send company representatives to countries on information seeking/gathering exercises. Subsidised travel and accommodation are usually part of the package organized by the sponsoring body.

Exporters do not make enough use of trade missions. This is probably because too few executives are aware of them and those that are do not understand their value. In many ways a well-organised mission gives you a first-class ticket to meeting prime contacts. Some trade missions are heavily subsidised, especially where DTI money is available.

Some of the best, from the point of view of organisation and results, are those run by the London Chamber of Commerce, particularly to the United States. Although few of these are subsidised by the DTI many are sponsored by leading organisations such as the National Westminster Bank.

The secret of their success and the reason why so many businessmen join the London Chamber's outward missions is the level of organisation and detail which goes into their planning. As Ian Weatherhead, Head of the Chamber's North American and Caribbean Section points out:

'A first-class mission organiser will:

- Organise contact events such as cocktail parties, lunches, dinners and seminars.
- Publicise and promote the mission in advance.
- Produce a list of prime prospects and in the case of the London Chamber will have opened the doors for contacts so you will not be going in cold.
- Assist in making appointments, and will often effect introductions and even accompany you on your initial visit – thus cutting down the unpredictability of a cold call.
- Create a good mix of delegates for a mission thereby ensuring a good interchange of ideas.'

Trade missions normally last for about one week. Groups are usually limited to between 10 and 20 people. Travel and accommodation is arranged either through the organizer or through an appointed travel agent.

Subsidies are given only when sponsorship is provided by the DTI.

Planning your participation in a trade mission – action checklist

- Set yourself a list of objectives to be achieved. Write it down so that you can check them off as you complete them. It is often the case that on a mission you get yourself so involved that you have neither the time nor the energy left to complete everything you set out to achieve.
- First of all do your homework. Your participation in the mission might be to collect information. Yet the better you have researched the market before you go the more productive will be the time you spend collecting new information or verifying that which you already have.
- Discuss the sort of people you want to meet and the places you want to visit with the mission leader. Ensure you have plenty of material to show contacts and prospects prepared in the language of the market you will visit.
- Check with the mission leader that Embassy Commercial Counsellors are aware of the visit and that the Central Office of Information has details of the mission's purpose. You should be able to channel information and PR material through to the COI ahead of your visit. If you have something really exciting to offer you might take the opportunity to get on radio or television.
- Find out from the mission leader (if information is not already supplied) what contact events are organised and what special dress might be required.
- Obtain a copy of *Hints to Business* from the DTI for general advice about the country.
- Before you finally embark make sure that you have a fair proportion of your appointments made, otherwise it may be difficult to organise a working diary when you arrive. Do not forget to take ample supplies of business cards!

10

Finding out what missions are available

Trade missions are listed in the *Trade and Industry Supplement*. If you are a member of a Chamber of Commerce (especially London and Birmingham) you will receive notification of outward missions that are being planned. Many trade associations and foreign Chambers of Commerce also advertise their missions in trade journals and in newsletters. It is worthwhile, therefore, writing to associations asking them to notify you of trade missions to countries in which you are particularly interested.

Exhibitions

Research shows that buyers visit exhibitions to:

- See new products and developments
- Obtain technical and product information
- Talk with and compare potential suppliers
- Find foreign companies for whom they can become local distributors.

Thus companies taking part in exhibitions have a unique opportunity to introduce themselves to or reinforce their relationship with customers and specifiers for their products.

Exhibitions are especially useful for building up contacts in foreign markets – particularly in Europe. Each exhibition you take part in should be part of a programme of activity designed to create a dialogue between your company and its potential markets.

An exhibition should be seen primarily as a selling medium. The objectives for participation in any exhibition should be associated with establishing customer and specifier contact, introducing product developments and opening a market for continuous sales opportunities.

Uses of exhibitions in the international promotional mix

The principal uses of exhibitions are to:

- Establish initial contacts in a new market through which longer term sales opportunities can be developed.
- Widen a company's contact and customer base in an existing market.
- Provide an opportunity to show and demonstrate products, processes and applications to specifiers and opinion formers (e.g. architects, engineers, etc.).
- Gauge initial buyer and trade reaction to new products and designs.
- Create a focal point to meet existing buyers and customers in an environment where they are receptive to new ideas and interested to see and evaluate their suppliers' offerings.

Exhibitions also offer opportunities to see and evaluate competitors' offerings and to meet trade and consumer media correspondents.

Use exhibitions as a promotional event

Exhibitions provide an element of theatre around which activities can be mounted to seduce visitors on to your stand to present them with your unique selling opportunity. Just setting up a stand and waiting for contacts to appear is undervaluing the role of exhibitions in your promotional mix.

Why do exhibitions fail?

The main reasons for a poor and ineffective exhibition are:

- Poor visitor quality. This means that either your target audience selection was wrong or the exhibition failed to attract the audience it promised to attract.
- Your stand was difficult to locate or visitors failed to notice it.
- Your stand failed to entice visitors on to it.
- The people manning your stand were ineffective.
- Your company had low recognition in the trade and was, therefore, not seen as a priority by visitors.
- That *follow-up* was not carried out effectively.

To the list above we can add further reasons, some of which are rarely recorded:

- Your stand was not ready on time thus losing valuable selling and demonstration opportunities
- Administrative bungling leading to literature being inaccurate, poorly translated or not available at all.
- Avance publicity was not carried out effectively.
- Exhibits were lost or stolen before or during the exhibition.
- Enquiry forms and visitor information records were lost during the packing away of the exhibition or in transit home.

10

Key criteria for a successful exhibition

You must ensure that all exhibitions, wherever they are run, are endowed with success criteria from the outset and this means:

- Defining your target audience.
- Using venues where your target audience is most likely to be reached.
- Creating 'theme and theatre' which attracts people to the stand.
- Avoiding stands that are difficult to locate or are hidden away from visitor traffic flow at an exhibition.
- Manning your stand with competent, well-motivated salespeople capable of conversing in the language of the country.

- Organising the exhibition in such a way as to ensure that its success is not spoiled by administrative errors.
- Establishing company and product recognition ahead of the actual event through advance publicity and PR.
- Having a pre-planned *follow-up* system to ensure that all interest shown by your contacts, potential customers, specifiers and journalists is exploited to the full.
- Setting a realistic budget and keeping to it.
- Exploiting the exhibition for news value.

Planning exhibitions

If exhibitions are to be effectively exploited to meet important objectives within the overall international promotional mix they have to be planned and organised with a great deal of creative and administrative skill. Thus, according to one of Britain's top exhibition and sales training companies – Anvil Dexter Ltd an accountable person needs to be assigned the tasks of:

- Defining objectives.
- Translating objectives into 'theme and theatre'.
- Finding suitable shows or exhibitions.
- Setting a realistic budget.
- Organising a promotion and publicity plan for the exhibition.
- Organising and coordinating exhibits, stand design and literature.
- Transporting all the materials needed from their assembly point for the exhibition together with administrating customs documents.
- Planning stand organisation.
- Pre-planning follow-up activity.
- Evaluating the effectiveness of the exhibition afterwards.
- Seeking and utilising government financial and administrative support.

Certain costs may be reclaimable under the various BOTB schemes available and information relating to these can be found through enquiring to BOTB at the addresses listed in the Appendix.

Promotional and publicity plan for the exhibition

Studies in the UK indicate that the average prospect has difficulty in visiting more than 131 stands in a normal day and stays up to 19 minutes on each. From personal experience, it is unlikely that this will vary much from country to country. You are thus in competition with other exhibitors for your prospects' valuable time and attention. The problem facing you as an exhibitor, therefore, is to find ways to ensure that both *key* prospects and an adequate flow of *high-quality* prospects are induced on to your stand.

The importance of an advance promotional and publicity plan in this respect cannot be over-emphasised, particularly where your company is still little-known by the target audience in a foreign market. Thus, the target audience needs to be carefully identified. Advertising techniques or direct mail should be used to inform and persuade the target audience to visit the stand. This activity should be coincidental to a planned PR campaign aimed at creating interest and awareness of the company and its products.

Exhibits, stand design and literature

You are recommended to adopt a *theme and theatre* approach to surround the exhibition event itself. Exhibits have to be selected in relation to the overall marketing plan and to individual opportunities which you have identified in the market selected. The 'theme and theatre' of the exhibition should be created around the products and should be reflected in the stand design and literature. The stand should be designed professionally (i.e. to a high standard), either 'in house' or through a design organization. The design brief should include the following:

- The 'theme and theatre' concept selected for the exhibition.
- The exhibits and demonstration equipment required.
- Corporate identity, logos and colours to be used.
- Regulations and prohibitions to be observed (as found in the exhibition organiser's contract).
- Stand location.
- Stand space plan.

10

Objectives

As with any form of business activity, there is a need to define intentions and objectives. Exhibitions are no exception. Yet a properly conceived exhibition is the product of a number of supporting activities and subsidiary activities built around the main event itself. In setting objectives, therefore, we are concerned with:

- The primary objectives of the exhibition itself, e.g. to recruit distributors, introduce new product lines, make contacts with specifiers.
- The supporting activity objectives which are concerned with attracting high-quality prospects to the stand.
- Subsidiary objectives to exploit opportunities for which the primary

and supporting activities create opportunities, e.g. reinforcing company and product recognition, PR, marketing information objectives.
- Training staff to sell competently and demonstrate products exhibited, etc.

Show or exhibition

The choice of show should be based on simple, if not obvious, criteria:

- Its location should be within targeted territories.
- The target audience of potential customers and specifiers should match the visitor profile.
- The show should have an adequate selection of good sites which ensures that exhibitors have a reasonable chance of attracting sufficient members of the target audience to their stands.
- There should be sufficient facilities to ensure that exhibits can be shown adequately (e.g. height, weight loading limitations, handling facilities, etc.)
- The organisation of the exhibition should be well regarded in terms of attracting visitors, managing security and low propensity to labour disputes.
- There should be adequate support facilities, e.g. telephone, fax, telex, information desks, feeding centres for staff, accommodation, etc.
- Supporting companies such as freight forwarders, stand builders and so forth can easily be found to handle the exhibition.

Major trade shows

Advantages

There are a number of specific trade exhibitions staged around the world. They attract regular exhibitors and, more importantly, regular trade buyers. Well established and renowned, as well as offering would-be exhibitors an abundance of data on visitors, traffic volume and other information, they are the principal focus for buyers and suppliers alike. Being the shop window of their industry, they are amongst the first choice of venues by serious exhibitors.

Disadvantages

Principal trade shows do, however, have their drawbacks for new, and especially foreign, exhibitors and a few are mentioned here:

- The industry's key suppliers will be there. Attracting the attention of, and being hospitable to, major buyers may be difficult and they may simply not have the time to visit newcomers.
- There is nearly always a ballot for sites and regular exhibitors will be given a weighting factor to ensure they are not allocated poor sites.
- Every major exhibition venue has its own peculiarities whether they be as simple as lack of accommodation or, more seriously, proneness to labour disputes, poor security or difficulties in handling.

Lesser-known trade shows

The smaller shows present greater difficulties but often have hidden advantages. For example, it was found in the US that buyers in outlying states were unwilling to travel to many major exhibitions. Many companies found in the US that buyers in outlying states were unwilling to travel to many major exhibitions. As a result they found that participation in more localised major state shows was far more productive in reaching a national audience than national shows.

Research

All *bona fide* exhibition venues should be able to provide data on the quality as well as the number of visitors attending their exhibitions. In Europe and the US the exhibition industry is so competitive that this service is now the rule rather than the exception.

The DTI produces considerable information through its various bodies and may also provide additional information through its Commercial Counsellors operating in its Embassies and High Commissions abroad. Where participation is encouraged by Trade Associations, Chambers of Commerce or the DTI, there is usually an abundance of data together with package deals and incentives.

Agents, distributors, advertising agencies and so forth can also be called upon to provide information.

Set a realistic budget

Exhibitions involve a considerable outlay. For an exhibition to be effective costs have to be planned realistically. The budget should be set to meet fully the costs of the exhibition and should be appropriate to the scale of the intended promotion.

The key areas to consider are:

- Research and advance visits.
- Cost involved in designing stand, literature, advertizing, etc.
- Cost of the stand and space.
- Constructing and dismantling the stand.
- Hire of furniture and services (e.g. telephone).
- Transport and insurance costs.
- Staff accommodation and travel costs.
- Cost of models, sales promoters and any special costumes needed.
- Give-aways and promotional activities.
- Advertising, direct mail costs, etc.
- PR and publicity costs, e.g. photography.
- Customer hospitality costs.
- Special services such as the cost of interpreters.

There should also be a provision to cover contingencies, mail and gratuities.

Design

A scale model of the stand should be produced to give a full impression of what it will look like when completed.

Literature will need to be designed and printed. You should have it professionally translated into the language of the country in which the exhibition is to take place. For important international shows (including those in the UK), other languages may also be necessary. For a show in say Frankfurt, German, French, Italian and English literature should be a minimum. Again, literature which is thematic to the overall event will add to the 'theatre' and later aid recall amongst your prospects.

Transport and customs administration

The transport of materials to an exhibition requires much the same documentation as for a normal export shipment. Yet it has to be remembered there is often no distributor's agent on the other side to clear the materials sent. (Unless of course a distributor is involved.) You will, therefore, have to organise your own clearing arrangements.

Materials may simply be shipped and forwarded through a forwarding agent or, alternatively, a contractor can be employed to take care of everything. In the US, however, clearing and forwarding are undertaken by two separate and distinct parties: the licensed customs broker and the appointed drayage contractor, respectively. Goods entering the US from abroad must be, in the first place, consigned to the customs broker before they are handed over to the drayage contractor. It is usual when shipping exhibition material for a bond or guarantee (carnets) to be entered into between the clearing agent and the local customs, thus permitting goods to be entered duty free (these can be arranged through your Chamber of Commerce). Provided goods are not sold and do not remain in the country beyond a specified period, no duty costs will be incurred. This means that you must liaise with either your agent or the customs authorities before materials are removed from the exhibition site for shipment back home.

Shipping can incur losses and damage to your goods and many experienced exhibitors would recommend the use of sealed containers. Regardless of the method used, all materials should be clearly marked.

Normal procedures for shipping insurance have to be followed.

Joint venture schemes

For first-time exhibitions abroad, joint venture schemes are highly recommended. Many joint ventures are organized by Trade Associations and Chambers of Commerce and are more often than not subsidized by the DTI/BOTB. This involves moving materials to a central destination at home where, with other exhibitors' materials, everything is assembled together and shipped in one lot. This method can take much of the administration work out of shipping materials and, through a group, costs may be saved.

10

Shipping

When goods arrive abroad in readiness for the exhibition, it may be necessary to store them for a short while. Some exhibition venues have facilities, others do not. It is important that you find storage space in advance. If the exhibition venue cannot accept the materials before a specific date, then other places need to be found and demurrage paid.

Shipping and customs clearance procedures add to the length of time needed between shipment and the exhibition date. Shipping by sea to distant countries incurring week's delay is still a good service, yet if goods arrive a week after the exhibition, then all is lost. Lead times, therefore, need to be on the generous side, for it is better for goods to arrive early and incur demurrage costs than for them to arrive too late.

Protection of patents and trade marks

When your company exhibits its products in alien markets, it exposes its technology and brand names. It should be understood that in many countries there are companies only too ready to take advantage of foreign companies which have not registered patents or trade marks. Some of them can work surprisingly rapidly. Your company should use patent and trade mark laws to protect itself. The old idea of simply using the words 'Patent Applied For' rarely works against companies which the trading community popularly dubs 'pirates'.

Stand organisation

As we revealed earlier, certain key elements of an exhibition have the potential to make or spoil a good event and none more so than the organisation of the stand and the people running it.

Personnel

The people running the stand have to be competent in product knowledge, have selling skills and be well motivated. At least one (preferably two or three) should have good linguistic skills. The manning levels should be planned in regard to the size of the stand, the number of prospects likely to visit it and the duration of the exhibition. A stand manager should be appointed and a roster produced to enable personnel to be rotated while keeping the stand adequately manned. Most importantly, all staff (including specially contracted staff and interpreters) should be thoroughly briefed and selling skills rehearsed. Furthermore, the organisation of customer hospitality and off-stand entertaining of targetted prospects should be planned.

Security

Security of the stand needs to be planned for. The loss or damage of exhibits, the stand itself or literature can spoil the event. Obvious precautions can be taken but someone has to be put in charge of locking things away and for checking and clearing each evening. For some exhibitions it may be necessary to employ the services of a security company. Dismantling the stand and removing exhibits provides lots of opportunities for theft and loss. Again, security precautions need to be taken, for apart from the loss of expensive exhibits, duty may become payable on items not re-exported.

Keeping records

Prospect enquiries need to be logged and records kept. The inadequate handling of these or their misplacement will greatly reduce the effectiveness of the exhibition. One tip is to produce self-carboning enquiry pads which enable you to keep two sets of records, one set with the stand manager, the other for follow-up. Later the stand manager's set can be used to check against the progress of follow-up activity.

Follow-up

Follow-up activity has to be pre-planned. Immediately on return, both people and time have to be allocated to follow-up leads. This has to be a physical activity calling on someone to return to the country to visit interested prospects. If this activity is delegated to agents or distributors, activities still have to be managed to ensure that all leads are effectively followed up.

There will be an inevitable delay between the exhibition and the time that prospects are visited. A mail shot could be sent to keep up the dialogue between the prospect and your company. This mail shot needs to be planned and produced in advance to ensure that it is sent out as soon as the exhibition is over. PR activity should not be overlooked and press releases covering newsworthy items should be organised and sent to the relevant media.

Evaluation

Needless to say, as with any other promotional event, you should conduct a formal evaluation. This serves three purposes: measuring the effectiveness of the exhibition in terms of sales and leads; measuring cost effectiveness and adherence to budget; and, finally, it is an experience record which can be used for future planning exercises (see J. Dudley *Successful Exhibiting*, Kogan Page, 1989).

10

BOTB services and exhibitions

The BOTB aims to reduce complications and cost for participants in exhibitions abroad. Through schemes designed to encourage groups of exhibitors sponsored by a recognised Trade Association or Chamber of Commerce, the BOTB will:

- Provide exhibition stands and display aids at a reduced cost.
- Assist with travel grants in some circumstances.
- Provide assistance for the cost of surface freight for exhibits.

British Pavilions are also organised at certain international fairs overseas by the BOTB. You should apply to the Fairs and Promotions branch of the Board for information. Again, stand, travel and freight subsidies are often available (see also *Successful Exhibiting*, J. Dudley, Kogan Page, 1989).

Conferences and seminars

International conferences and seminars are often sponsored by companies or in conjunction with international bodies. Companies involved in this sort of activity are usually based on high technology. For instance, conferences and seminars are a favourite medium of pharmaceutical companies in creating and marketing a dialogue with the medical profession the world over. Such conferences, on specific areas of medical science or therapeutic areas of interest, such as the International Congress of Rheumatology, are largely industry-funded.

Companies in specific industries may also run seminars, training courses and so forth on a local basis. These, of course, can be on a grand scale and dubbed with the title 'National', or can be a localised series of events involving relatively small groups of people. Rentokil, for example, helped build its international reputation through lectures and demonstrations which were well publicised in the local media and supported by the information services of the British government's Central Office of Information (COI) and the external services of the BBC.

International medical, transport and tourism conferences tend to take the form of congresses where important users and opinion-formers are invited. Usually the host country to the congress provides a Minister or two to give the occasion some legitimacy. Companies which either sponsor or participate in these conferences have to be very subtle and not over sell their products unless, as in the case of pharmaceutical companies, a congress is called to discuss a product as a medical breakthrough.

Organisation of international events of this kind tend to be the responsibility of either the PR or the sales promotion department. Again, like exhibiting, they require considerable groundwork, planning and preparation. Such events not only have to achieve objectives specific to them but should contribute generally to the international news output from the organisation.

Store promotions

The British government helps promote British goods in certain centres by giving stores promoting the goods a contribution towards promotional expenses. There are only a limited number of venues per year and these are listed in the *Trade Promotions Guide*.

Store promotions offer only a limited opportunity for serious exporters in that unless they form part of an overall marketing plan, their infrequency and limited locations provide little scope for developing a sustainable promotional programme (between 1983 and 1986 the BOTB ran an average of 23 per year). They are, however, useful:

- as a short-term promotional event for an existing major retail outlet
- as part of the promotional activity for a particular territory
- as an opportunity to build business in a major outlet.

However, on its own the scale of a limited retail promotion is insufficient to build or develop a market and in a retail environment crowded with other British products, it is difficult for any single product to stand out.

British weeks

British weeks were considered very much a joke in the 1970s but in recent years have once again become more popular. Again, like store promotions they are very much 'one-off' promotions and are likely to favour existing exporters rather than new ones.

Participation in British weeks can be useful at the introductory stages of market development and should be integrated into a territory's promotional activities together with involvement from your distributors and your own promotional activities.

The table below gives details of government support for missions, exhibitions, seminars and store promotions over recent years.

Type of event	Average no. of events (1984–7)
Overseas trade fairs	305
Overseas seminars	33
Store promotions	23
Inward missions	59
Outward missions	148

Source: B TB

10

11   Contracts

Shipping terms □ Covering the buyer's risk □ Covering your risks □ Assessing your risk □ Methods of payment □ Methods of managing foreign exchange risk □ Cargo insurance

Contracts are important. All too often after a deal is made the contract is a secondary issue, the terms either being dictated by the buyer or following an existing system adopted by the firm. If buyers specify the type of contract they want, it is usually because there is some financial benefit in it for them. If it is important for the buyer to specify the type of contract, then it must be important for the seller too.

Let us, therefore, review the elements of a contract to establish the benefits and weaknesses of different elements. A legal contract involves three key criteria:

- an offer
- an acceptance
- consideration (payment)

Without all three criteria, then a contract is not legally binding. An export contract, therefore, has to clearly state the offer, the price and the means of payment. The buyer has to agree and accept the terms offered before the contract is legally binding. Even so, safeguards need to be introduced to ensure that:

- Risks of the transaction are covered.
- Documentation is correct.
- Procedures by the exporter and importer ensure that the contract and payment is not affected by customs frustrating or otherwise hindering the export/import processes or seizing the goods altogether.
- Ownership of goods passes from seller to buyer at a recognised point in the transaction.

A traditional export contract therefore includes:

- A description of the goods.
- A price.
- A point or destination at which the ownership of goods passes from the seller to the buyer.

- Responsibilities for carriage and insurance.
- The method by which goods will be despatched.
- The documents required by the buyer.
- Bonds and guarantees.
- The method, period and currency of payment.
- The seller's bank through which payment is to be conducted.
- The name of an arbiter should there be a dispute over a contract.
- Details of which party is to be responsible for bank charges and so forth.

The contract will, therefore, encompass the movement of goods, documentation and a financial transaction.

The way the contract is formed will affect the benefits, risks and often the relative levels of duty raised on the transaction. It is, therefore, critical to:

- Study the pros and cons of each element of the contract.
- Understand the effects different contracts may have on customs duties and procedures.
- Ensure risks to both buyer and seller are minimised.

Export contracts historically revolve around shipping terms, insurance and methods of payment. Thus the three requirements of the contract involving price, ownership and responsibilities for insurance are covered in shipping terms.

Shipping terms

CIF

11

CIF stands for Cost, Insurance and Freight. Where goods are sold on CIF terms, you (the exporter) are responsible for insurance cover and frieght to an agreed port of destination. The invoice covers the cost of these services.

The *advantages* to you (the exporter) of CIF contracts are:

- You can choose the shipping company to meet whatever cost, reliability and service criteria you require.
- The insurance of goods in transit rests with you. Thus, if goods are lost or damaged on route, you make a claim and receive settlement directly from the insurers. This often overcomes delays by importers in settling accounts on goods not delivered intact or lost. It also overcomes any

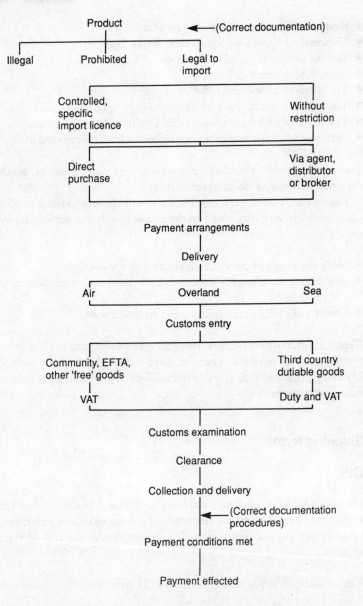

Fig. 11.1 Scheme for planning an export transaction contract and documentation. *Adapted from a framework devised by Setform Ltd (copyright holders)*

reluctance on behalf of central banks to release funds for insurance on goods not received (where there are foreign currency regulations).

The *disadvantages* to you (the exporter) are:

- The freight and insurance costs absorb working capital against which there is no profit contribution made. The longer settlement dates are set, the longer funds are tied up unprofitably and the greater the risk to currency fluctuation.
- Where your customers can find cheaper freight costs, then your prices quoted to include CIF may be viewed by the importer as uncompetitive.
- Organising CIF arrangements is somewhat more demanding in terms of people and time than FOB for example, purely because insurance and freight have to be negotiated.
- Such arrangements may not suit your customers, who may be marshalling stocks from various exporters in a country in order to ship them in bulk to their own warehouses in their own country.

The *advantages* to the buyer are:

- He is totally aware of the total costs incurred in the contract from factory gate to receipt at port of entry.
- The responsibility for loss of goods or damage in transit rests entirely on the shoulders of the exporter. Thus all the buyer has to do is to place a fresh order on the exporter who will have all the trouble of making insurance claims.

The *disadvantages* to the buyer are:

- He may wish to make individual arrangements for importation which may include bulk shipping of several manufacturers' products.
- He may wish to risk less satisfactory means of transport to reduce costs.

FOB

FOB stands for Free on Board. Where goods are sold on FOB terms, you (the exporter) are responsible for all costs and responsibilities for goods until they are put on board a ship or aircraft. In effect, the buyer takes possession of the goods once loaded.

The *advantages* of FOB terms to you (the exporter) are:

- It is quicker and easier to calculate an offer price to the customer.
- The buyer takes possession of the goods before actual shipment and is thus contractually responsible for payment regardless of what happens to the goods.
- It may suit the buyer.
- You (the exporter) do not have to finance freight and insurance beyond the point of embarkation.

The *disadvantages* to you (the exporter) revolve around the problems of securing insurance payments from the customer should the goods go astray or be damaged.

The *advantages* for the buyer are the discretion he can exercise in selecting shipping companies and insurers and the control over the shipment which this entails.

The *disadvantages* to the buyer are:

- He has to finance the cost of freight from time of shipment. Any delays or demurrage fall automatically on to him.
- He is entirely responsible for handling insurance claims which may tie up working capital whilst claims are being settled.
- Any mistakes in documentation made by the seller (whilst reclaimable later) have initially to be sorted out by the importer, as ownership rests with the purchaser.
- Problems and disputes are left with the buyer to sort out. Whilst this may in theory be an advantage to you (the exporter), the friction and costs may damage the relationship between seller and buyer, to the seller's long-term disadvantage.

EXW

EXW refers to Ex Works terms. Here the buyer takes costs and responsibility quite literally from the factory gate. All the seller is expected to do is to pack the goods and make them ready for collection. No costs of freight or insurance of cargo are necessary.

The advantages for the seller are thus somewhat greater than FOB, as the cost and time required in preparing shipping and insurance arrangements are saved.

Often EXW terms apply to customers who marshal goods from several suppliers for onward shipment to their own markets. Well-organised buyers using their own export houses will insist on this type of arrangement. The costs saved can either be passed on by the importer for competitive pricing or retained as additional contribution. The advantages to the buyer are thus obvious.

Risks to the exporter do however arise, especially where the buyer is relatively unknown. The reason being that it is not at all uncommon for buyers to divert shipments to markets where the seller had no intention of letting them go. A breed of export entrepreneurs from both home and abroad have learned to buy in bulk at export discounts (especially with large cash transactions) to ship goods to markets where they undercut the exporter's appointed representatives. The effect is to undermine prices in those markets. This is one of the ways in which 'parallel traders' operate. Not all transactions are strictly legal where the buyer circumvents duty or VAT in disposing of the goods. It is, however, difficult for sellers to avoid such transactions, for the 'professional' parallel trader is all too well acquainted with European Community Law. This law, in effect, debars companies from restricting the sale of goods to specific customers in an attempt to reduce competition.

It is also important to note that EC legal constraints covering competition cover all transactions in the Community regardless of whether the goods are to be shipped outside the Community.

FAS

FAS stands for Free Alongside Ship and refers to terms which mean that the goods are transferred to the buyer before the goods actually go over the side of the ship. It is similar to FOB but it does mean that the importer is responsible for demurrage and loading. The advantages and disadvantages to both parties are more or less the same as for FOB.

Although hair-splitting cases covering legal disputes between buyers' and sellers' insurers have been brought before the court, to decide ownership where it was essential to establish whether the goods were actually over the side of a vessel or not, they have decided disputed ownership in FOB terms. With FAS terms such (uncommon) cases would not arise.

FRC

This stands for Free Carrier and is exactly the same as FOB except that you (the exporter) deliver to a carrier at a named point. FRC has been designed to meet the requirements of 'multi-modar' transport such as containers or 'roll-on, roll-off' traffic.

FOR/FOT

These stand for Free on Rail and Free on Truck. You (the seller) are responsible for the goods until they are loaded on board a railway wagon or truck. Thereafter, as with FOB, the buyer is responsible.

DCP

This relatively uncommon term stands for Freight Carried Paid To, which means that you (the exporter) pay for carriage of the goods to a named destination but are not responsible for insurance. The key disadvantages of this type of transaction are that you have no control over insurance and it is debatable where ownership actually changes. It could be reasonably argued that as the buyer is insuring the goods, then you (the exporter) are acting as a contractor in moving goods owned by the buyer.

CIP

Again, a less commonly used term which stands for Freight Carriage and Insurance Paid To. This is the same as DCP with the exception that you (the exporter) are responsible for insurance. You are responsible, therefore, for goods until they arrive at a specific destination. This type of contract is not to be recommended where you have to take care of import procedures on behalf of the customer.

INCOTERMS

All of these terms follow international rules, so that their meaning is commonly interpreted all over the world. The principal delivery terms are set out in *INCOTERMS* which is obtainable from its publishers, the International Chamber of Commerce, British National Committee, Centre Point, New Oxford Street, London, WC1A 1QB.

Covering the buyer's risk

Buyers' risks have to be taken into account. Very often companies who tender for export contracts find that the conditions of a tender require a bank guarantee. This is usually on a percentage of the value of the tender – and is normally five per cent. You will have to obtain a guarantee from a bank – this is known as a 'tender bond'.

If and when you are awarded a contract you may subsequently be required to underwrite performance by providing a guarantee of say five or ten per cent of the value of the tender. This is known as a 'performance bond', and will remain in force until the contract is completed. You are normally released soon after the issue of the performance bond.

The issue of tender and performance bonds indicates to the foreign buyer your financial standing. The purpose of these bonds is also to act as a safeguard should the contract not be carried out satisfactorily. Bonds or guarantees are often required to cover advance payment and retention.

Bonds and guarantees are arranged by banks and should you be involved in a transaction which demands a guarantee then you must get advice from the international department of your bank.

Covering your risks

Your risks in an export transaction involve:

- Defaults on payment by the importer.
- Failure of the importer to obtain foreign exchange.
- Fluctuations in exchange rates.

You will need to find ways of reducing these risks. It is important therefore to consider them at the contract stage. You have a number of choices which are appropriate under different market conditions.

Action checklist – assessing your risks

- What risks apply to each given transaction in terms of customer standing, foreign exchange regulations prevailing in the customer's market and the present level of exchange rate volatility?
- What mechanisms can be used in the transaction to limit the potential risk?
- What insurance cover can be obtained to cover risks and what will it cost?
- What is the level of risk you are prepared to take given the costs of lesser-risk options?

11

Your basic market research and customer credit status information (from Dunn and Bradstreet) will help you estimate the risks involved with the customer's status and the prevailing foreign exchange controls in the customer's market. Your bank will be able to help you assess your foreign exchange risks, but in a turbulent world this is considerably more difficult. The dynamics of the world money markets can make rapid and unexpected short-term shifts in relative currency values.

Evaluate the following sections in order to create for yourself a set of options most likely to reduce risks and the costs of insuring against them. The following sections cover:

- Methods of payment
- Methods of managing foreign exchange risk
- Credit insurance
- Cargo insurance

Methods of payment

There are three basic methods of payment. Each is listed below, in order of increasing risk.

Advance payment

This is often quoted as the best method for the exporter. It is a method often used for unsolicited business from unknown buyers, yet the advantages to the exporter outweigh the disadvantages to the buyer who will have to tie up funds in advance of delivery. Furthermore, advance payment provides no guarantee as to the final destination of the goods purchased. Other methods, as we will see, at least ensure that goods are cleared into the country to which they are destined.

Where advance payments are made guarantees or bonds may be required by the importer.

In practice only a very small proportion of export sales are conducted in this way.

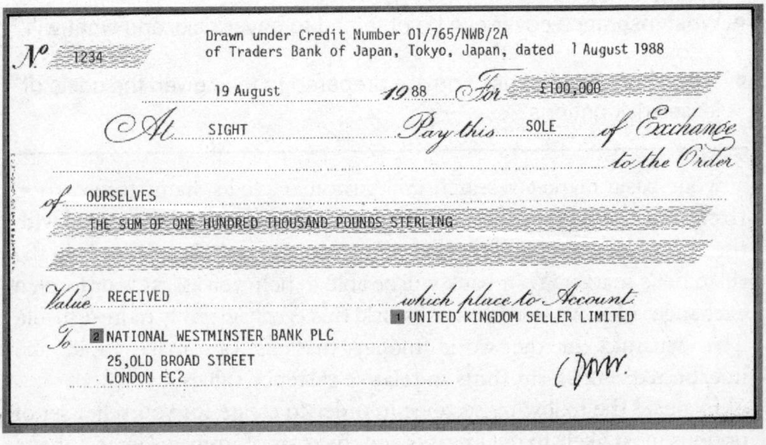

N? 1234

Drawn under Credit Number 01/765/NWB/2A
of Traders Bank of Japan, Tokyo, Japan, dated 1 August 1988

19 August   *19* 88   *For*   £100,000

At   SIGHT   *Pay this*   SOLE   *of Exchange*
to the Order

of OURSELVES

THE SUM OF ONE HUNDRED THOUSAND POUNDS STERLING

Value RECEIVED   *which place to Account*

UNITED KINGDOM SELLER LIMITED

To NATIONAL WESTMINSTER BANK PLC

25,OLD BROAD STREET
LONDON EC2

(DWW.

Fig. 11.2 Specimen bill of exchange. *Reproduced by courtesy of the National Westminster Bank PLC*

Documentary credits

The next most secure method of payment is through a Documentary Letter of Credit, which in simple terms can be defined as:

> A written undertaking given by a bank on behalf of the buyer, to pay the seller an amount of money within a specific time, provided the seller presents documents strictly in accordance with the terms laid down in the letter of credit.

In effect the buyer provides the seller with guarantee of payment in return for an assurance from a bank that the required export documents have been delivered to the bank's satisfaction.

Types of documentary credit

Terms such as 'irrevocable' and 'revocable', 'confirmed' and unconfirmed' are used to describe different types of documentary credit. Let us therefore describe each.

Irrevocable and revocable letters of credit distinguish between documents which allow the obligations to alter. Irrevocable documentary credits are more commonly used. The term 'irrevocable' means that the obligations of the parties to the credit cannot be altered without the agreement of all parties. This is a source of protection to exporters.

Revocable credits can be cancelled or amended by the importer (opener) or the importer's bank (opening bank) at any time until payment negotiations or acceptance have been made by the advising (paying) bank.

Confirmed and unconfirmed documentary letters of credit distinguish between documents confirmed by a bank which the exporter can reliably be assured will guarantee payment of the letter of credit.

An unconfirmed letter of credit is subject to the issuing bank's ability to provide the necessary foreign exchange at the time the documents are presented. In countries where foreign exchange is restricted, local banks may be unable to acquire sufficient foreign exchange to meet the obligations of a letter of credit. Countries such as Nigeria, for example, still have large outstandings of unconfirmed letters of credit which local banks were unable to meet with foreign exchange.

Where the advising bank adds its 'confirmation', it guarantees that provided all the terms and conditions of credit are strictly complied with, payment will be made irrespective of what may happen to the issuing bank. Common practice therefore is to ensure that letters of credit are confirmed by a British bank. Increasingly, however, international banks in

③ **National Westminster Bank PLC** ♻

International Banking Division
Documentary Credits Department – Overseas Branch

---

④ United Kingdom Seller Limited
Baltic House
27 Leadenhall Street
London EC3

Dear Sirs

We have been requested by ② Traders Bank of Japan, Tokyo, Japan to advise the
issue of their irrevocable Credit Number |01/765| in your favour for account
① of JAPAN BUYER CORPORATION c/o NYK Line 3-2 Marunouchi 2-Chome, Chiyoda-ku,
Tokyo 100, Japan for £100,000 (SAY ONE HUNDRED THOUSAND POUNDS STERLING).

⑤ available by your drafts on us at..XXXX..sight accompanied by the
following documents namely:

⑤ 1. Signed Invoices in triplicate certifying goods are in accordance with
Contract No. 1234 dated 23 July 1988 between Japan Buyer Corporation
and United Kingdom Seller Limited.

⑤ 2. Marine and War Risk Insurance Certificate covering "all risks" warehouse to
warehouse, for 10% above the CIF value, evidencing that claims are payable in Japan.

⑤ 3. Complete set 3/3 Shipping Company's clean "on board" ocean Bills of Lading
made out to order of the shippers and endorsed to order of "Traders Bank
of Japan", marked "Freight Paid" and "Notify Japan Buyer Corporation c/o
NYK Line 3-2 Marunouchi 2-Chome, Chiyoda-ku, Tokyo 100, Japan".

Covering: Mechanical Spare Parts CIF Tokyo, Japan.

Shipped from UK Port to Tokyo, Japan.

Partshipment prohibited   Transhipment prohibited

Documents must be presented for payment within 15 days from the date of shipment.

We are requested to add our confirmation to this Credit and we hereby undertake
to pay you the face amount of your drafts drawn within its terms provided such
drafts bear the number and date of the Credit and that the Letter of Credit and
all amendments thereto are attached.

The Credit is subject to Uniform Customs and Practice for Documentary Credits
(1983 Revision), International Chamber of Commerce Publication No. 400

Drafts drawn under this   [X] Payment
Credit must be presented to us for [ ] Negotiation } not later than 14 September |1988
                                  [ ] Acceptance

and marked "Drawn under Credit Number 01/765/NWB/2A of Traders Bank of Japan,
② Tokyo, Japan   Dated 1 August 1988

Note: On the grounds of security the above Credit, whilst accurate in content, is used for illustrative purposes only.

---

1 Buyer/Applicant   4 Seller/Beneficiary
2 Issuing/Opening Bank   5 Documents Required
3 Advising/Paying/Confirming Bank

Fig. 11.3 Specimen documentary credit. *Reproduced by courtesy of the
National Westminster Bank PLC*

strong currency markets are used by exporters for confirming letters of credit.

As a UK exporter, you will gain the maximum security of payment through having the confirmation of a leading UK bank on a documentary credit.

Open account

Where an established buyer–seller relationship exists and where foreign exchange availability is not a problem, then business can be conducted on an open account basis. Competitive pressures frequently make this a necessity.

This method of payment is naturally the highest in terms of risk. It is therefore essential that you trust customers whom you intend to trade with on open account and mark credit limits very carefully – both in terms of exposure and time period allowed.

How you will obtain payment is also important even on open account terms. Legal procedures required abroad to enforce payment under open account arrangements are more complicated than those to enforce payment of a letter of credit. Whilst a buyer's cheque is a perfectly good instrument for transferring money the expense of clearing it together with the risks of it being returned as a result of some technical irregularity or through lack of funds is high.

It is probably less risky and cheaper to ask the buyer to make payment by banker's draft or through the buyer's bank by mail or telex. It is worth remembering that postal delays can occur and so it is beneficial to have funds transferred by telex – especially for larger amounts. The cost of the transaction is usually low compared to the cost of a delay. It is worthwhile quoting your bank's name, address and account number on your invoices to save correspondence and to avoid mistakes.

Importers favour open account trading because it enables them to plan their cash flow, and make payments cheaply with the minimum of formality. You should avoid open account trading with customers located in countries where foreign exchange is highly regulated. It has become apparent over the years that where countries such as Nigeria have run short of foreign exchange, documentary credits are given priority in the queue for allocations.

Methods of managing foreign exchange risk

Trading in sterling

Historically, UK exporters have invoiced their customers in sterling. This has evolved out of the tradition that sterling, being one of the world's major currencies, was, to the beginning of the Second World War, one of the two trading currencies of the world. Things have changed. Buyers are no longer prepared to accept the risks of being invoiced in a currency other than their own in a world of volatile exchange rate fluctuations.

The key advantages of invoicing sterling for UK exporters are that the customer bears the risk and that necessary expertise does not have to be brought in to the small business to manage foreign currency transactions. Yet by invoicing in sterling, as an exporting company you can put yourself at a severe marketing disadvantage. If exchange rates turn against the buyers' advantage then most will increase their prices to their customers and demand will fall.

Secondly, where the currency advantage passes to a customer prices become distorted if the customer uses the additional saving to be passed on as discounts. Within markets supplied by a number of different export customers this could mean that there will be several different selling prices in a market for the exporter's products, as each importer will have bought goods at different times and at different exchange rates. It could also mean that any discounts arising because of exchange rates could be used to finance parallel trade.

Trading in the importer's own currency

The advantages of quoting in the importer's own currency are that whilst the exporter bears the exchange risk, market prices can be kept fairly stable. It will also help the buyer to manage selling prices in the longer term rather than trying to predict prices for each shipment. It should also be stressed that in good inventory management importers should be attempting to match selling prices to the costs of replacing their inventory. Thus any severe and adverse change in exchange rate, no matter how short term, could result in their increasing prices of existing inventory rather than awaiting new shipments at new exchange rates.

A further complication arises where the buyer prefers to pay in a third currency. Here you have the risk of fluctuating exchange rates reducing both your own and the buyer's profitability.

Key issues in managing foreign exchange risk

Whilst many financial experts will argue for and against different foreign exchange policies the two issues you need to be especially aware of are:

1. The impact of price fluctuations on your market.
2. The effects of exchange fluctuations on your own company's profitability.

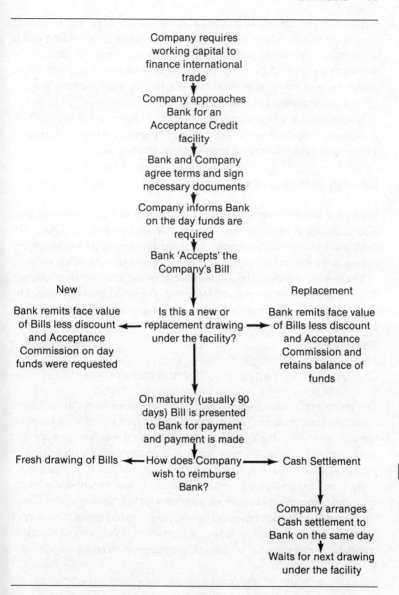

Company requires
working capital to
finance international
trade

Company approaches
Bank for an
Acceptance Credit
facility

Bank and Company
agree terms and sign
necessary documents

Company informs Bank
on the day funds are
required

Bank 'Accepts' the
Company's Bill

New   Replacement

Bank remits face value   Is this a new or   Bank remits face value
of Bills less discount ◄── replacement drawing ──► of Bills less discount
and Acceptance   under the facility?   and Acceptance
Commission on day   Commission and
funds were requested   retains balance of
                                                     funds

On maturity (usually 90
days) Bill is presented
to Bank for payment
and payment is made

Fresh drawing of Bills ◄── How does Company ──► Cash Settlement
                       wish to reimburse
                       Bank?

Company arranges
Cash settlement to
Bank on the same day

Waits for next drawing
under the facility

Fig. 11.4 Acceptance credit facility in operation. *Reproduced by courtesy of the
National Westminster Bank PLC*

The danger, of course, is in being overly concerned with the second of
these – the impact of currency movements on individual transactions –
where the real problem is ensuring the development of your market.
Whilst the ups and downs of exchange rates tend to balance themselves

out over time, fluctuating market prices may have an extremely weakening effect on your market in the long term. The overriding aim as always is to worry about your market and its development rather than the short-term effects of currency movements. Whilst you may lose some margin in the short term it is vital not to lose your markets and the investment you have made in them.

It is essential in planning export contracts to have a knowledge of how foreign currency deals work. Yet it is also important for you to take expert advice from your bankers on how to cover against risks.

Dealing in foreign exchange

Banks will always quote two prices for a current or 'spot' exchange rate. The bank will always buy high and sell low against sterling. That is the bank will look for more currency units against the pound sterling when buying and offer less foreign currency per pound sterling when selling.

There will, therefore, be a difference between the two rates offered. This is known as the 'spread' and represents the bank's profit margin. The daily and financial press publishes exchange rates. Remember they represent yesterday's closing rates and that the selling rate is always quoted first.

Can you protect against exchange rates?

The problem of transactions involving two currencies is that their relative conversion rate changes. Thus a price agreed, say, six months ago based on the rate prevailing for the conversion between a foreign currency and sterling may be quite different when it is converted back on receipt of payment. Sometimes it will be more than expected, at other times less.

So how do you guard against losses? There are basically three approaches you might evaluate for suitability for your own business. These will depend to a certain extent on your spread of markets and frequency of transactions, your own 'in-house' expertise in international financial transactions and the level of risk you are prepared to take.

Where you have many markets and frequent transactions

Frequent transactions across a number of markets enable you to provide a range of markets against which to reduce risks. In effect you will have a 'basket' of currencies against which to average out your currency gains and losses. A sophisticated approach would be to apply the moving average exchange rate to each of your markets, thus enabling you to make planned price adjustments.

However, where a disproportionate amount of sales or where risks are especially severe in an individual market, you may be better advised to isolate the transactions and protect them using forward exchange contracts, as explained in the next section but one.

Where you have frequent transactions in very few markets

Here again the frequency of transactions may average out your currency gains and losses. However, you may wish to forecast an average moving exchange rate against which to make adjustments to the price you charge your customer, the aim being to smooth price adjustments so as not to upset your prices in the foreign market concerned. However, where risks are forecast, the safest route is to make forward exchange contracts.

Where you make infrequent or seasonal transactions

Here it is difficult to balance risk. One way, of course, would be to operate currency accounts where you would buy an equal value of materials from the market. If this were possible you would balance your risks exactly. It is certainly a technique used by larger, sophisticated organisations with a regular two-way flow in a given currency and if applicable to your company would be worth evaluating.

The other option would be to make forward exchange contracts. This, however, involves a premium on your exchange rate quotation. It pre-empts the fall in relative values of currencies. It may provide windfall profits, but this is not the point of the exercise, for what you in fact are doing is passing the exchange risk to the bank for a predetermined cost.

Forward exchange rate contracts are legally binding agreements between a bank and its customers. The contract ensures that the currency is exchanged at some future time at a predetermined value.

You (the exporter) are protected from an adverse currency movement for once a contract is entered into it does not matter how much the current 'spot' rate of exchange may vary between the time of entering the contract and its maturity. This is because you have negotiated a fixed rate with your bank. Covering currency risk on a forward basis thus provides a form of insurance and is a prudent step where currency exposure could threaten the profitability of transactions.

A forward exchange contract can take two forms. It either (1) specifies a fixed future date or (2) provides an option for the customer to deliver or take delivery of the agreed currency within an agreed time. The option in a forward exchange contract, unlike a stock exchange option, is not one offering a choice as to whether to exercise it or not. It is an option which concerns only the *timing* of the delivery when one currency is exchanged for another.

11

The way in which banks arrive at forward rates is to take the current spot rate and add a 'premium' or 'discount'. The calculation is based on interest rates. Thus if you enter a forward exchange contract for your pounds against a currency with a lower interest rate than sterling, you would expect it to be at a premium against sterling. Conversely, one with a higher interest rate against sterling will be at a discount. Premiums are deducted from the spot rate and discounts are added.

If you approach the bank to sell a currency which commands a premium for sterling at a date in the future, you will be quoted a lower rate than the present spot rate. For example, if a UK exporter sells goods valued at Swiss Francs 100,000 and expects payment in three months:

	Bank sells	*Bank buys*
Spot rate	SF 2.6790	SF 2.6840
3-month forward rate	0.0450	0.0450
	(premium)	(premium)

the exporter enters a forward contract to sell SF 100,000 in three months time:

Spot rate	= 2.6840
Less 3-month premium	= 0.0450
3-month forward rate	= 2.6390

Thus at the forward rate, the exporter will receive £37,893 – compared to £37,258 at the current spot rate of 2.6840. However, an importer buying SF 100,000 will find that it costs him £37,965 at the forward rate of 2.634 (2.6790 – 0.045) compared with £37,327 at the spot rate of 2.6790.

ECGD

The ECGD (Export Credits Guarantee Department) covers around 30 per cent of all exports from the UK and 80 per cent of standard or near standard goods made in the UK through its network of regional offices (see Appendix 4). It has paid out some £2bn over the last two years, preventing many exporting firms from liquidation.

ECGD covers both buyer risks and country risks. Under its various policies you can cover your normal 'off the shelf products' with short-term guarantees. ECGD is also unique in providing pre-shipment cover against goods made to specification for a special customer or specific market requirement. There are a variety of policies covering royalties on licensing, franchising agreements, sales through subsidiary companies, constructional works contracts, goods sold after export, etc. There is a multi-sourcing endorsement for the short-term guarantee which gives cover for UK manufacturers and merchants dealing in foreign goods and UK merchants trading goods or commodities between other countries.

Extended-term guarantee cover is also available for goods sold on terms of longer than 6 months or which take more than 12 months to manufacture. Cover is also available for a wide range of currency transactions as well as policies for additional losses in meeting forward exchange committments. Whilst guarantee packages tend to vary, you can access ECGD cover for either all your export business or perhaps only

0–6 months	6 months–2 years	2 years–5 years	5 years
Bank loans – Sterling/currency (dependent upon availability) Overdrafts/ negotiations	Bank loans – Sterling/currency (dependent upon availability)	Bank loans – Sterling/currency (dependent upon availability)	Bank loans – Sterling/currency (dependent upon availability)
Small Exporter Scheme	–	–	–
Insured export finance	Insured export finance	–	–
Joint Policy Plan	Joint Policy Plan	–	–
Confirming finance	Confirming finance	Confirming finance	Confirming finance
Export factoring	–	–	–
Invoice discounting	–	–	–
–	Forfaiting	Forfaiting	Forfaiting
Receivables financing	Receivables financing	–	–
–	–	ECGD supplier credit ECGD buyer credit	ECGD supplier credit ECGD buyer credit
–	–	ECGD general purpose line of credit	–
–	–	ECGC project lines of credit FINCOBE (similar but through finance house)	ECGD project lines of credit FINCOBE (similar but through finance house)

Fig. 11.5 Export finance facilities offered by the National Westminster Bank PLC. *Reproduced by courtesy of the National Westminster Bank PLC*

11

specific parts of it. However, ECGD are unlikely to cover high-risk 'one-off' transactions unless they are offset by a portfolio of lower risk transactions.

You can deal direct with ECGD or you can take up one of the many packages offered by export finance organizations which incorporate ECGD cover. You should talk to export finance companies or your international bankers to work out the best package for you.

Whilst it is true that you are paying a premium for risk cover, you do have peace of mind in knowing that your investment in developing export markets is not being undermined by either buyer or country risks. Remember, however, that ECGD only covers about 90 per cent of your risk.

Role of confirming houses in financial risk management

Confirming houses, as pointed out in Chapter 6, can play an important role in financial risk management. By acting as a buyer's agent, confirming houses provide 'non-recourse' finance. They take on risks which it is very often difficult to find finance for from other export finance institutions, and have a knack of finding lines of credit for their customers in high-risk corners of the world.

Cargo insurance

It is important to have some grasp of the basic principles of cargo insurance, although you are best to consult your insurance broker for detailed advice.

The two essential points to remember about cargo insurance are:

- You must ensure that goods are insured at every point between the time they leave your warehouse until they are safely delivered to you customer.
- You must establish for which parts of the journey the responsibility for insurance of the goods rests with you and which parts rest with your customer.

The differences between a CIF and FOB contract, therefore, become important when the matter of insurance arises. This is discussed in full at the beginning of the chapter, but to recap CIF means you have to insure the goods all the way because you are paying for the freight – your customer does not in fact take possession of the goods until the destination stipulated on the contract is reached. FOB means you have no further liability for goods once they pass over the side of the vessel carrying them – here it is the responsibility of the customer to insure the goods for the rest of the journey. It is important, therefore, that you and your customer reach an agreement on the terms, methods of shipping and insurance.

Insurance and documentary credits

The 'conditions' clauses of a documentary credit will cover insurance. It is absolutely vital that your insurance strictly complies with the conditions of the documentary credit. Failure to do so will hinder the payment process.

Insurance value

The purpose of insurance is obviously to recover the value of the goods should they be lost, damaged or destroyed. In most cases goods are insured to cover:

- their value (plus 10 per cent)
- the cost of freight.

Should you need to make a claim then you will receive either the whole amount of the value if goods are lost or damaged or a proportion only of the value if they are damaged. If they are damaged beyond economic repair, then the goods will be written off under the provision of 'total constructive loss'. However, where this occurs the underwriters have the right to whatever remains of the original goods and the right to dispose of them.

Risks to be covered

11

You can insure your goods for almost any risk – given you are prepared to pay the premiums demanded. The exceptions are, however:

- You cannot insure against damage which is inherently probable because of the nature or composition of the goods (e.g. propensity to go off or attract odours).
- You cannot insure unlawful cargo.

These exceptions come under the heading of 'inherent vice'.

In recent years underwriters have set out a range of fairly standard insurance packages. Under the heading *Institute Cargo Clauses* produced by the Institute of London Underwriters, insurance is listed under three clauses – A, B and C.

- Clause A is an 'all risks clause'.
- Clauses B and C provide only basic insurance for shipments which are relatively low risk.

Exclusions

All Institute cargo clauses exclude:

- War risk.
- Damage due to strike.
- Riots and civil commotions.

It is important to examine the exclusion clauses for all cargo insurance so that you know exactly what you are covered for.

Where you are excluded from CIF cover

There are around thirty countries, as well as most of the communist countries, where you cannot sell on CIF terms. Where you are trading with these countries on a confirmed irrevocable documentary credit, your liability stops the moment the goods pass over the side of the vessel. You need to be careful when shipping to these countries that you are not lulled into a CIF arrangement, where you are forced to take out insurance in the destination country. The reason for this is that whilst goods are insured it may not be possible to obtain remittances of foreign exchange. When trading with these countries take specialist advice on insurance.

Carriers' liabilities

All carriers have a legal responsibility of custodianship. A body of common law stipulates that carriers exercise a reasonable amount of care. The general principles governing custodial care are subject to a number of treaties, viz.

- Road – CMR Convention conditions.
- Air – Warsaw Convention.
- Sea – Hague Visby Rules.

Insurance options

Cargo insurance is normally underwritten at Lloyds of London or the major insurance companies. There is no need to take out a separate policy for each shipment. The insurers provide a facility of open cover or open policy. This enables you to write your own insurance certificates without having to inform the insurer in advance. You are, however, under an obligation to inform the insurers of every shipment you make.

Insurance certificates as part of shipping documentation

The insurance certificate is an important document needed to complete the full set of shipping documents. It is essential if the importer – or anyone else who has an insurable interest to whom the certificate can be endorsed – is to make a claim.

Making a claim

Claims need to be notified within 60 days for sea transport and 30 days for air. The claims process is advised by the insurer but usually involves:

- Obtaining a survey report from the insurer's agent.
- Forwarding the survey report together with all relevant shipping documents (invoices, bills of lading, or airway bill, and the certificate of insurance), plus a claim in writing against the carrier or other party who is responsible for the loss.

Again, your broker is probably better informed and equipped to handle your claims.

11

12 Logistics management for exporting

The effect of the structure of distribution channels on the logistics system □ Transportation difficulties and costs □ Warehousing □ Inventory management □ Time lags □ Customer service □ Methods of transportion □ Sea □ Documents of international trade.

Shipping, transport and distribution can be grouped under one heading, Logistics. Logistics planning involves not only the transportation side of distribution but also provides the 'place element' in the marketing mix by helping to ensure that products arrive in sufficient quantities in saleable condition at points where the consumer can most easily buy them. Thus, logistics management includes forecasting demand and matching supply to meet that demand through procurement of materials, production scheduling, inventory management, order processing, warehousing and transportation.

In international systems the logistics planning function involves a number of sub-systems which have central points for each territory. There is a further sub-system for the management of local logistics, i.e. the transport and distribution systems used by the importer to move your products to customers in the market concerned.

Logistics, as well as being essential for moving goods to their destinations, is also a key marketing activity. As such it requires marketing management's attention. Logistics contributes to a major portion of costs, particularly in international business. Logistic planning also plays a major role in creating a good relationship with customers, ensuring that sales opportunities are not lost because of stock outs (which allows competitors to eat away at the company's market share).

The effect of the structure of distribution channels on the logistics system

Every market has its own distribution problems; Few resemble each other in the composition of channel structure. In most less developed countries the channel structures are difficult, with goods passing through many intermediaries before reaching the final consumer. In Western developed countries channels tend to be shorter, yet even in Europe trade structures and buying methods vary considerably. In the US the grocery market is dominated by multiples and co-operatives; Finland has few stores *per capita* because of the predominance of general stores; Italy has a fragmented retail and wholesale structure. In the Netherlands buyers having co-operative ventures among retailers to carry out wholesaling operations is quite common.

In Kenya, for example, government regulations prohibit direct sales to retailers without wholesale licences. Wholesale and retail structures therefore vary between different countries. For each territory it is important to be aware of the logistics system's cost of operation and efficiency in providing the 'place element' in the marketing mix.

Transportation difficulties and costs

Transportation costs are often peculiar in that they frequently bear little relation to distance. The key factors in cargo pricing are competition and volume. For example, goods going from the Far East to the East Coast of the USA pay less than 30 per cent of the rate of goods going the other way. Costs from the USA to South America are frequently lower than among South American countries.

In planning transportation the problems can be enormous and considerable hidden costs can be concealed; e.g. the costs of out-of-stock positions which lose you business, or delays over insurance claims which you have to finance. As one sarcastic client of mine commented, 'When you need the goods they get lost or delayed. When you are overstocked they arrive six weeks early!'.

In assessing the real cost of transportation you should be concerned with factors relating to reliability, time and price. Therefore, your decisions in choosing methods of transport and distribution will be based on 'trade-offs' between these factors.

12

Warehousing

The importance of stock or inventory management should not be underestimated in the context of international marketing management. Many large multinational organisations and large exporting companies have their own warehouses in their key markets but this is not always really economic for smaller companies, many of which simply cannot justify the ownership of warehouses in their markets.

The exporter may enjoy facilities offered by the distributor, joint venture partner and so on, but there can be advantages in using public warehouses. The bonded warehouse allows for imported products to be stored and duty is not payable until goods are physically moved from the warehouse (in most cases).

Another idea not uncommon in many countries and those heavily dependent upon entrepôt trade is the *free zone* which, in addition to the services available from the bonded warehouse, offers no limitation on the storage period and allows for product exhibition and sale. Free zones are springing up all around the world close to sea and air ports.

Inventory management

Inventory control calls for a number of skills which enables management to maintain sufficient stock in the market without causing stock outs and which, at the same time, does not overburden the company's working capital by tying up too much stock for too long.

In essence you are looking at two interacting systems: demand, which is pulling goods through distribution channels to meet demand, and supply which maintains adequate supplies to meet demand. The demand system is influenced by promotion, prices and product inputs of the marketing mix, and the supply system is based upon sourcing and grouping goods.

It is, and always will be, a problem to forecast demand accurately. The ideal is to be able to control export distribution systems well enough to achieve the exact balance between over-stock situations in the distributor's warehouses and stock-outs occurring in the market. Most exporters try to increase stock holdings in the distributor's warehouses and the distributor

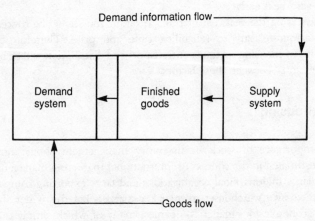

Fig. 12.1 Integrated supply/demand system

connives to achieve minimum stocks. The problem will remain, of course, that stock-outs mean lost sales and, for high demand products, frequently lead to further problems of parallel importing by other distributors and wholesalers. Furthermore, competitors may well take advantage of such a situation to introduce a competitive product.

Inventory management is thus concerned with pooling sufficient stocks to meet demand in each market. Where goods are made in one market and shipped to another you are really concerned with a dual system. Inventories are held both inside and outside the market, the idea being to feed an inventory from one without over or understocking the other.

Time lags

Time lags are a major constraint on flexibility for exporters. Not only do you have to take into consideration the time factor in shipments, but you also have to look at other delays in the system, such as order transmission and processing, packaging time, and time taken to clear goods through sea and airports and Customs. The following example illustrates the problem quite clearly:

- Customer decides to place order.
- Request for pro-forma invoices is made.
- Pro-formas are prepared by the exporter.
- Pro-formas are returned to the customer.
- Import licences are requested.
- Import licences are received.
- Order confirmation is sent to exporter.
- Exporter instructs warehouse to consign stocks.
- Warehouse packs stocks.
- Shipping arrangements are made and documentation prepared.
- Goods are transported to sea or airport.
- Goods are cleared through the port.
- Goods are loaded onto vessel or aircraft.
- Goods are shipped to port of entry.
- Goods are unloaded
- Goods are cleared through port.
- Goods are cleared through Customs.
- Goods are transported to customer's warehouse.
- Goods are unloaded and received into customer's warehouse.
- Goods are inspected and transferred to customer inventory.

This list roughly describes the sequence of events in processing an export

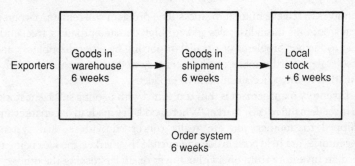

Fig. 12.2 Order system

order. Long as it is, this could take up to two months from start to finish given that there is no breakdown in the system or errors, e.g. by the shipper or transporter.

It is critical that the levels of inventory be geared to the time lags in the system. A system which takes, say, more than six weeks to complete means that no less than six weeks' stock can be carried in the market, given that goods are already in shipment.

In the system shown above a six week inventory in the market demands that where it takes, say, six weeks to ship them, a new order has to be placed as soon as stocks are received in the local warehouse. It does not take a mathematical genius to show that such a system is likely to result in stock-outs from time to time due to any break down in the process.

Customer service

Customer service is the logistical support of customer orders and its principal features are:

- Delivery time.
- Special delivery instructions.
- Order processing and documentation.
- Materials handling.
- Information service.
- Special order handling.

If a marketing approach to logistics planning is adopted, then customer service standards are set first and costs are minimised. If customer service is considered as a constraint on the logistics system then the financial benefits are those of weighing the opportunity cost due to not meeting customer needs on the one hand with savings in the logistics costs on the

other. Surveys around the world point to the following as being essential
to customer service:

- Product availability.
- Order status.
- Local distribution.
- Delivery time.

The consequences of poor customer service manifest themselves in:

- Lost sales.
- Potential de-listing.
- Future de-listing.
- Actual de-listing or a lack of support for future activity.

The principle of logistics support is the linking of the customer demand
and company supply loops, Figs. 12.3 and 12.4, taking into consideration
the vital questions of how complex the interacting loops are between the

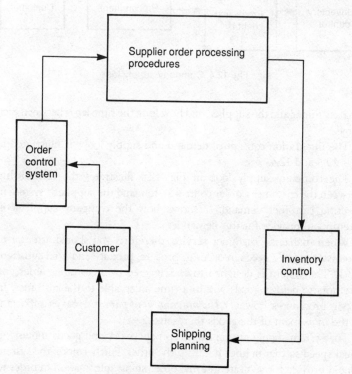

Fig. 12.3 Customer demand loop

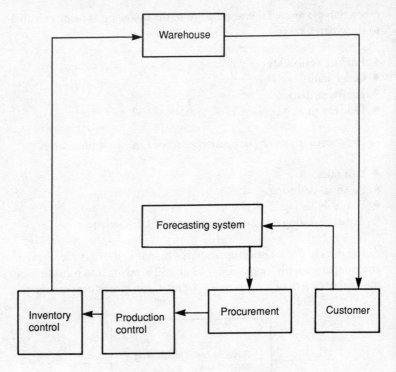

Fig. 12.4 Company supply loop

final customer and the supplier, and how long the time lag is between each stage.

The integration concept of demand and supply loops is illustrated in Figs 12.3 and 12.4.

The company supply loop in Fig. 12.4 illustrates the relationship between the customer's order control system and the supplier's system in meeting customer demand. It shows how the company supply loop attempts to provide for this demand.

When managing customer service, therefore, you should attempt to forecast customer needs in order to procure, produce and hold sufficient stock. The system is designed to be triggered by a customer order and attempts to deliver goods within a time acceptable to the customer. In export procedures, however, *the movement of paperwork* is as important as the movement of the goods themselves.

The system should attempt to keep paperwork and goods moving at equal speed so that neither holds up the other. Furthermore, the system should provide for accurate internal order status information in order to answer enquiries from your customers. Whereas lateness of an order can cause a certain amount of irritability amongst customers, inaccurate or unreliable information on order status can cause severe problems in maintaining good customer relations. The system should also be flexible enough to take care of special delivery instructions and order handling.

In the final analysis good customer service is critical in maintaining good relationships with customers. It is necessary to evaluate a system both by its level of cost and its effectiveness. This starts first by assessing the point below which opportunity costs in terms of lost business or loss of customer support begin to outweigh savings and secondly, by calculating the point at which costs cease to obtain further benefit.

The skills in managing the demand and supply interactions initially come from accurate demand estimates, and then from good logistics management which uses forecast information. Modern personal computers are easily programmed using inexpensive software to process demand information and sourcing requirements. In this technological age there is no excuse for the processing to be done by hand.

Methods of transportation

Mail
Road
Rail
Air
Sea

Mail

One of the easiest and most convenient ways of moving small items around the world is by mail. For parcels up to 10 kilos there is minimal documentation and little handling of parcels required by the sender. The mail is used by publishers, drug companies etc., where small quantities can be sent with a degree of security to virtually any destination. This method of transporting goods is also particularly useful for samples and small amounts of promotional material, e.g. catalogues and leaflets. By avoiding warehousing, etc., it does mean that a parcel can be sent directly to the intended recipient without it having to pass through goods inwards departments and so on. Furthermore, it can be used to back up a spare parts service for small but expensive items such as camera parts. This avoids the problems involved with distributors having to hold large stocks of expensive parts – particularly where the service and spares side of the operation is not one from which the distributor makes a profit. However, it must be borne in mind that not all postal systems in the world are as

12

good as those in the UK. Take your distributor's or agent's advice on the suitability of post as a means of delivery. If the post is an insecure method in a territory – *do not use it*!

Road

Companies use road transport extensively both domestically and externally, particularly in Western Europe, although road routes are opening up further destinations. The growth of roll-on/roll-off facilities by cross channel road ferries in Britain and the European continent, for instance, has stimulated a growth in this means of transport. It is not uncommon for British vehicles to travel as far as Turkey and beyond. Limiting factors in the UK are the maximum sizes of vehicles permitted on the roads.

The movement of vehicles across Europe is greatly improved by the dropping of internal tariffs and bonding procedures for *en route* countries, as well as the use of the TIR system (Transport International Routier). This allows vehicles to be sealed in one country, which reduces customs procedures to a minimum at the destination port or customs posts.

Developments in the use of 'compatible' trailer-loads is growing in Europe. The system depends on a trailer being shipped on its own to a European port and then collected by a compatible towing vehicle. This reduces the problems involved with licensing, insurance, foreign traffic regulations and means, of course that the home-based drivers spend less time away from home.

The great advantage of road transport, where it can be used with whole loads or, at least, limitable pallets, etc., is that a firm's products can be shipped direct from the factory to the customer without any need for intermediate unloading and wharfing, etc., thus reducing unnecessary delays – as well as mitigating damage and pilferage.

Rail

Rail services are a highly competitive alternative to other means of transport. Rail seems to become more economical the further the distance that goods are transported. Rail transport is inexpensive, and the main costs and inconveniences (particularly for short haul routes) stem from transporting goods to and from terminals. Some systems are efficient and few delays are experienced, but it must be remembered that transporting goods for considerable distances overland may subject them to the extremes of the weather. For example, trans-Siberian railways can be subject to considerable delays in winter and goods are subjected to very low temperatures – in summer they face high ones. For certain cargoes, these railways can be a less expensive method of transport to the Far East than shipping, although goods take considerably longer to arrive and may have to be handled several times.

Freight liner systems

In the UK the freight liner system is developing into a very efficient domestic transport system. In the past the drawback has been compatibility of rolling stock with foreign systems.

Lift-on/lift-off

A significant development in transportation is the growth of compatible lift-on/lift-off wagon containers. They allow for speed and ease in moving goods by road, rail and boat, and can be very competitive with roll-on/roll-off systems, and other road transport.

Here again, however, we have to look at benefits apart from cost when comparing systems, to quote from Mark Wronski's Cranfield Monograph: ...

'When companies are planning unit loads to Europe they are faced with the choice of either using containers or roll-on/roll-off vehicles. To reach a decision based on the principles of total distribution, the mere cost benefits of one over another do not suffice ... Amongst the other factors to be taken into account in the decision are the product mix and how it affects the density of the shipment, the length of the haul and associated relative cost rates, protective packaging costs, handling costs and customer benefits.'

Air

Many companies do not even consider air cargo simply because the rates seem prohibitively non-competitive compared with other modes of transport. Yet for certain markets and product groups the costs of holding inventories and buffer stocks may outweigh the cost advantages of less speedy means of transport. For high value, low bulk products, actual rates may be competitive; for perishable, expensive products (such as oysters, orchids, certain drugs and vaccines) no other transport system is fast enough over long distances.

Even where air cannot be justified on a cost basis and where its other benefits do not outweigh the additional costs, firms will use other systems for their day to day business, resorting to air cargo as an emergency measure only. There is, however, good reason to consider the use of air in certain areas of customer service,e.g. supplying of samples or providing a special replacement service. The former ensures that samples are received promptly and quickly, updating the customer's product knowledge, etc., as new products are introduced. This is particularly important if older designs are becoming obsolete and where sending samples by air can reduce the lead time for the selling of a new product. Even a few weeks saved in the early stages of a new product can substantially cut the payback period, as well as reducing competitors' reaction time. The latter parts replacement service could well become an air-oriented service. Whereas the direct costs of the service may increase because of the cost of air transport, the two advantages of not having to hold high stocks of replacement parts in the market and the maintenance of customer satisfaction may well outweigh the costs of the transport. Furthermore, if the customer is aware that replacement parts are being especially flown in for his benefit it may well help to create a favourable impression for the firm in his eyes. The situation where a customer has to wait months for a vital part for his machine, TV or car, etc., should be avoided for obvious reasons.

Air freight costs are by and large fixed by IATA (International Air Transport Association) but it should be remembered that there is often a large surplus of air cargo space for many destinations. To a number of markets, air transport costs are highly negotiable. Furthermore, IATA's general rates are based upon existing product groups and established routes and so new product groups going to new destinations may present a reasonable negotiating base for the firm and the air transport company.

Future developments in costs of air services and their availability will undoubtedly change in the future because of demand and advances in aircraft technology. Long haul air routes will no longer present a need for aircraft to make frequent stops *en route*, thus reducing overall costs. This, together with a more market-oriented approach by airlines to gain more cargo business by systemized rate charging and marketing, will cause a major change in world transport in the next few years.

There are already developments in air and sea systems whereby part of the route is covered by air and the balance by sea (or *vice-versa*). Whereas such systems are limited in application at present, future development may be significant.

Air transport can be booked under three headings:

Direct airline bookings

Here, the freight forwarder books space for the 'first flight available'. The rates are controlled by IATA and it is the quickest and consequently the most expensive way of shipping by air.

Consolidations

Freight forwarders can cut your air freight costs where they group together shipments from a number of their clients. These are then offered to the airline as a single cargo and prices negotiated accordingly. You can normally expect this method of air shipment to take longer than direct airline bookings but is usually less expensive. If, however, you plan for such shipments with your freight forwarder, there is a fair chance that there will be little difference in shipping time than with direct bookings.

Charter

This involves chartering a whole or part of a cargo plane. As you can imagine, this will be a considerable load, and is the most frequently used method for large shipments.

Sea

Sea transport is the traditional means of moving goods between countries which have accessible seaports. Considerable developments are being made in shipping in response to the increasing competitiveness of other modes of transport. Few industries in the Western, Communist and developing world are as politically sensitive as shipping. Despite the fact that there is over-capacity on some routes, the Communist bloc and many developing countries have, until quite recently, been increasing the size of their fleets.

Traditional sea transport

Excluding oil and other bulk primary products, few firms distribute sufficient of their products to any single destination to occupy the total cargo space in a modern vessel, thus most cargoes are mixed.

The shipping line has the problem of ensuring that the density of the 'mix' makes up a commercially viable load for each vessel. Complicated rate fixing procedures based on the cubic dimensions of the load and its weight have to be used to ensure that there is an economic distribution of space and displacement.

In an attempt to regularize rates and limit price competition for different types of loads, the consent of *shipping and liner conferences* have been set up for the various lines. These conferences are made up of associations of companies regularly serving particular routes. Whereas

12

price competition is restricted amongst members, deferred rebate schemes are available for regular customers.

Like any other form of cartel there is competition from companies and privately owned vessels which are not members of a shipping conference who offer competitive rates. Notable examples are vessels returning to 'home ports', anxious to attract cargo to avoid the costs of returning empty. Some domestic shipping lines do not belong to conferences for political reasons. The future of shipping conferences may be limited by the pressure being brought to bear by the US Federal Marine Commission and the competition regulations of the EC.

The main problems of traditional shipping methods are:

- The time taken in shipment.
- The need to book shipments well in advance of sailing dates.
- The threat of industrial action to disrupt progress of the goods, e.g. port labour disputes *en route* or at the final destination.
- Delays caused by goods being held up on wharfs. In fact in certain ports some officials are known to increase their stipends illegally by expediting cargo held up in the wharfs and sometimes holding it up until the necessary bribe is paid.
- The danger of damage and theft occurring *en route* where containers are not used.

Despite the problems, as a means of reaching most destinations sea transport is frequently the best and cheapest method available.

Containerisation

Containers have created something of a revolution in sea cargo traffic. The advantage of containers is that they are compatible to road and rail transport systems. If you can muster the necessary 16 or so cubic metres of volume to fill a container, you can be assured that (unless it is opened for customs examination) that your goods will arrive in good condition.

The role of the freight forwarder

Estimates suggest that some 70 per cent of cargo from the UK goes through the hands of freight forwarders. If you are new to the export business then use a freight forwarder for all non-mail transport.

The main services offered by freight forwarders are:

- Acting as your agent in the shipping process.
- Recommendation and selection of carriers.

- Preparation of documentation (legal instruments and bank documents).
- Packing and cargo supervision (as required).

Use your forwarding agent as a consultant to help you develop your logistics systems.

The freight forwarding business, like any other, is full of good and bad companies. They can be big multi-service organisations or highly flexible, narrow-niche businesses specialising in types of customer, cargo or transport systems.

When you select a forwarder bear in mind three factors:

1. Can you build a relationship?
2. Does the freight forwarder's size, systems and specialization match your needs?
3. Is the candidate company competent? (A reasonable indication is membership of one of the several freight forwarding trade associations, such as the Institute of Freight Forwarding.)

It is as well to get to know a few such organisations through meetings and visits to their premises before making a final selection.

Remember, however, that by using a freight forwarder's facilities and skills you can take a great deal of the administrative pain out of exporting, as well as making savings on internal resources. There is sufficient competition in the industry for you to both shop around and 'fire' any company which repeatedly lets you down.

Documents of international trade

If there is a side to exporting likely to create headaches, it's documentation. Each of the four transactional aspects of exporting require certain documents. Documentation is something you must get right if your goods are to reach their destination, be properly insured, pass through customs (both in the UK and at port of entry), and if you wish to receive payment! The papers you will need include:

- Various instruments used to obtain payment.
- Commercial documents relating to the sale and specification of goods.
- Receipts issued by transport operators and freight forwarders.
- Official documents designed to meet customs and licensing authority requirements.
- Documents relating to insurance.

12

As goods go through the export process, they need documents to overcome the various hurdles placed in the way of their free movement by customs and border controls. Whilst these are destined to be removed within the European Community in the next year or two, they persist today as elsewhere in the world.

Unless goods and documents are correctly connected there will be problems at three critical stages in the export process, namely:

1. Difficulties with HM Customs.
2. Delays or even confiscation of goods at the customs in the port of entry.
3. Delays in payment because of either inaccuracies in the documentation or problems clearing and obtaining the necessary customs stamp.

Buyers from abroad will often specify the documentation required. If this is not the case, information can be obtained from your local Chamber of Commerce, embassies, and consulates in the UK. *Croners Reference Book* for exporters also contains all the information you will need.

Simplifying matters

Over recent years there has been pressure to simplify export documentation. Ahead of Europe's Single Market new legislation has made redundant some 70 different forms through the Single Administrative Document. 'SAD' was introduced in 1988. It was used for all intra-Community trade and with many of the countries importing from and exporting to the Community.

SITPRO, the Board for Simpler International Trade, is an independent agency founded in 1970 and endorsed and sponsored by the DTI. Its aims are to make British firms more competitive abroad by attacking red tape and advancing the use of information technology in the trading, distribution and payment processes.

Documents

Invoices

These can be drawn up in several different ways, depending on circumstances. The most frequently found are:

Commercial invoices are the supplier's invoices required by the buyer. You will need at least three copies, legalised by a Chamber of Commerce or a foreign consulate. They will need to be made out to meet HM Customs requirements and in a format specified by the importing country – for use by their customs authorities.

Your invoices should contain:

- A full description of the goods.
- Details of shipping and packaging marks as they appear on the bills of lading.
- The price of the goods.
- Details of the terms of contract (see pp. 127–32).
- Details of freight and insurance costs where payable.
- Details of import licences and exchange permits where applicable (double-check that your invoice does not exceed either the quantity or value of goods stated in the import licence or foreign exchange permit).
- In some cases, separate weight lists and specifications.

Certified invoices and certificates of origin. It is often necessary to certify that the terms of the contract have been fulfilled and specified for the country of origin.

There may be a requirement for certification to be carried out by an 'authorised' Chamber of Commerce, a list of which can be obtained from the Association of British Chambers of Commerce in London or from the Export Development Division of the Department of Trade and Industry.

Consular invoices are required by some importing authorities and take the form of specially printed documents obtainable from consulates. They *must be completed* in accordance with requirements.

In many cases a 'legalised' commercial invoice (i.e. stamped by the relevant consulate) will suffice. Remember, however, that obtaining 'legalized' invoices can involve quite long delays. You should begin processing these documents early when completing a transaction where this requirement exists.

12

Transport documents

Bills of lading

These are vital documents in the export process. A bill of lading serves three key functions:

1. It is your receipt from the shipping company for goods accepted for carriage.
2. It is evidence of a contract between your company and the shipping company and carries an understanding by the latter to deliver the goods in the same condition as they were received.
3. It is the document of title to the goods.

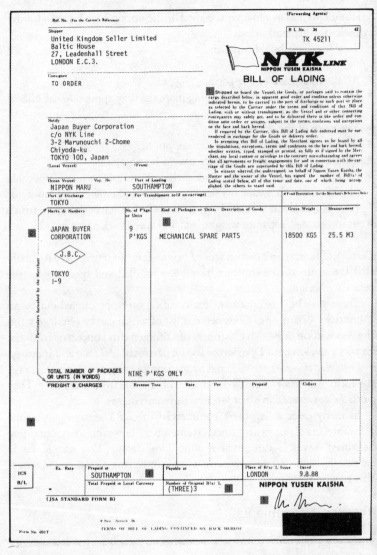

1 'Shipped on Board.'

2 Shipping marks.

3 Number of bills of lading in the set.

4 Transportation charges have been prepaid in line with the sale contract terms which are CIF.

5 Signed by, or by an Agent on behalf of, NYK.

6 Description of Goods should be consistent with the other documents.

7 Freight charges as calculated by the shipping company.

Fig. 12.5 Specimen bill of lading

The bill of lading is prepared by the exporter or the freight forwarder. It should contain a description of the goods, the terms of carriage, the name of the vessel and the port of discharge. It is then signed by the shipping company and issued in sets of one or more.

It is essential that the goods arrive at the shipping company in good condition. If they are damaged or badly packed the shipper will refuse to issue a 'clean' bill of lading – without which your buyer may refuse to accept the goods. If the shipping company has reason to believe there is a defect in the goods or their packaging the bill of lading will contain a clause to this effect: such bills are known as 'claused' or 'dirty'.

Your foreign customer will require you to produce bills as evidence that goods have been 'shipped on board'. When a bill of lading simply states 'Received for Shipment' there is a risk that the goods are lying on the dock awaiting the next vessel.

Title to the goods passes from supplier to buyer on endorsement and delivery of an original bill of lading.

The shipping company will only release goods at their port of destination against the 'original' bill of lading. It is therefore essential that proper control is exercised over these title documents.

When you ship goods on CIF and C&F terms you must ensure that freight is paid and that bills of lading are marked accordingly.

Airline bills

Airline bills are not documents of title. They are receipts issued by an airline for goods sent by air. Once goods have been cleared through customs, the consignee can claim them without further formalities.

Railway consignment notes

Again, these are not documents of title. They are receipts for goods transported by rail to an overseas destination.

Insurance certificates and policies

You must insure goods for export at every stage of their journey from your warehouse to the time the customer takes delivery.

Whilst export insurance requires expert advice you should:

- Ensure that you are covered to at least the full value of the goods. Most exporters insure for more than full value – usually 110 per cent.
- Cover the following risks: transport from your warehouse to the docks

PHOENIX ASSURANCE PUBLIC LIMITED COMPANY
Regional Marine Office Freshford House Redcliffe Way
Bristol BS1 6LX

Exporter's
Reference 91011

Certificate of Insurance No. 045826

This is to Certify that the PHOENIX ASSURANCE PUBLIC LIMITED COMPANY has insured under Policy

No. 20035A issued to National Westminster Insurance Services Limited

for account of United Kingdom Sellers Ltd &/or subsidiary &/or Associated Companies

who hereby declare for Insurance under the said Open Policy Interest as specified below so valued subject
to the terms and conditions of the said Open Policy and to the special conditions stated below and on the
back hereof.

Conveyance Nippon Maru From Southampton

INSURED VALUE: One Hundred and Ten
(in words)................. Thousand Pounds

Via/To   To   Tokyo

Figs: £110,000 Currency: Sterling

Marks and Numbers

Interest

JAPAN BUYER
CORPORATION

Mechanical Spare Parts
in 9 P'kgs

‹J.B.C.›

TOKYO
1-9

Institute Cargo Clauses (A)
Institute War Clauses (Cargo)
Institute Strike Clauses (Cargo)
Institute Classification Clause

The holder of this certificate is entitled to the above-mentioned insurance by virtue of a policy effected for and on behalf of
the holders of this and other certificates, and this certificate (subject to the special terms and conditions printed or written
thereon) will, for the purpose of collecting any loss or claims, be accepted as showing that the holder is entitled to the
benefit of such policy to the extent herein set forth.
In the event of loss or damage for which the Company is presumed to be liable (see also overleaf), immediate notice must
be given to:—

Claims payable by:— British Insurance Group (Japan)
P.O. Box 357
Kokusai Building
No. 1 - 1 Marunouchi 3 - Chome
Chiyoda-Ku
Tokyo

Consignees are reminded that cover under
this Certificate expires in accordance with
the Transit Clause in the Institute Cargo
Clauses.

PHOENIX ASSURANCE PUBLIC LIMITED COMPANY

Group Marine Manager & Underwriter

Dated at 8 August 1988

Signed

PU 188/82   This insurance is subject to English jurisdiction

1 Insured value is 110% of the CIF value
of the shipment.

2 Shipping details, marks and description
of the goods should be consistent with
the other documents.

Fig. 12.6 Specimen insurance certificate

or airport, storage whilst awaiting loading, the time spent aboard ship, road, rail or aircraft; final transport to the buyer.

You might also keep in mind the need for an extension to the policy should delay occur at any stage in transit.

Other important documentation

Certain goods and destination countries will require a variety of different documents. Those below are some of the more commonly encountered.

Certificates of quality and quality control

These may be required by your customers for any of the following reasons: assessment of duty; required document in the process of authorizing foreign exchange (e.g. some African countries); to cover bilateral arrangements whereby an importing authority will accept the company's quality control documents rather than having its own inspectors make the necessary inspections (e.g. pharmaceutical products).

ATA carnets

These are issued for goods to be exported on a temporary basis, e.g. to trade fairs or exhibitions, or for samples or special equipment which will be reimported. ATA carnets are bonds (issued through larger Chambers of Commerce) to enable goods to pass through customs without payment of duty.

Blacklist certificates

These documents provide evidence that goods do not originate from a list of countries from which the importing country has banned trade. Such documents may also require statements regarding the registration of the carrying vessel, and often, the ports of call prior to delivery.

Dangerous goods

These are subject to stringent packing, handling and carrying regulations. All forms of transport have their own regulations regarding carriage. Advice is available from the Dangerous Goods Advisory Service (DAGAS), Laboratory of the Government Chemist, Cornwall House, Stamford Street, London SE1 9NH.

12

Bills of exchange

The legal definition of a bill of exchange is 'an unconditional order in writing addressed by one person to another, signed by the person giving it, requiring the person to whom it is addressed to pay on demand, or at a fixed or determinable future time, a sum certain in money to, or to the order of, a specified person or to bearer'.

Bills of exchange are widely used in international trade as a means of claiming payment by the supplier (drawer) from the buyer (drawee) and can be used as a vehicle for obtaining trade finance.

13 Recruitment, management and motivation of distributors

Recruiting distributors □ Finding distributors □ The screening process □ General agreement of terms □ Appointing the distributor □ Drawing up the contract □ Motivation and development □ Support and training □ Mutual commitment to build the market □ The common element in excellent distribution □ Changing poor performers

Whether you appoint a traditional distributor or enter into some collaboration with a compatible firm in a joint marketing arrangement, whether distributors are expected to play a major or minor role in your export business, their recruitment, management and motivation will be key activities in ensuring successful business development in the territories where they are employed. It would be naïve to think that finding the right distributor is easy.

Some 80 per cent of British exports from the manufacturing sector of the economy go through distributors. There are few companies exporting products which do not use distributors in some or all of their foreign territories.

A distributor is usually:

- situated in the market designated;
- allocated distribution rights to a territory but not necessarily a whole country;
- actively involved in the marketing of the principal's products through sales management and, to varying degrees, marketing promotion and after sales service; and
- buys on its own account and gains income from the resale of its principal's products (sometimes a commission is added).

Companies often deserve the distributors they have. Those which fail to set recruitment, management and motivation policies rarely succeed in getting the best out of the market.

Your export operations will benefit from your recognising that a successful distributor network is based on:

- *Recruiting* distributors who are capable, effective and backed by sound contracts.
- *Managing distributors* in terms of communication, business planning, promotional activities and careful monitoring of results against performance criteria.
- *Motivating* distributors through sharing risk, incentives, public relations and training.

Recruiting distributors

The ease with which a company will find and appoint a suitable distributor in a territory will be influenced by:

- The image and reputation of the company.
- The availability of good distributors in the territory.
- The presence of competitors in the market who have already appointed better distributors.
- The potential for the company's products in terms of turnover and profitability.
- The company's terms.

Finding distributors

It is crucial that only the best possible distributors are appointed. Regardless of how important or how small a market is, the distributor must be responsible for getting the best of it for the principal. It is also important for principals and distributors to get on with each other – interpersonal chemistry should form part of the selection criteria for an agent. Many seasoned internationalists will point to one or two key people within a good distributor's organisation as being the main reason why relationships and performance are so successful.

Locating new distributors is not as difficult as finding the good ones. Within most experienced export departments good names are often well known to managers responsible for territories. Yet with newer export organisations this may not be the case. Managers then have to do a certain amount of research to find possible candidates. The following list gives sources of information.

- Consultant services can be employed to seek out and recommend candidates. This means that the task will be carried out very professionally and quickly, although it will involve costs (for which grants are often available.)
- Government sources such as the British Overseas Trade Board (BOTB) in the UK provide lists of contact addresses and further help through British embassy staff.
- Trade associations and chambers of commerce build up numerous contacts through the work they do in organizing trade missions and trade fairs, etc.
- Advertising agencies will often find leads for their clients through their international links.
- Trade missions, both inward and outward, provide opportunities for managers to find and make contacts.
- Personal recommendation from *bona fide* trade contacts can be an extremely useful way of finding potential candidates as long as the final choice is based on the candidates' credentials matching the selection criteria.
- Candidates can also be found through advertising but this does reveal the company's intentions to the market and usually leads to a considerable number of 'waste of time' applicants which have to be sifted out before a short list can be drawn up.
- Contact similar manufacturing companies (without directly competing products) to find potential candidates willing to enter a joint marketing arrangement.

The screening process

The aim of the screening process is to find a short list of, say, three or four candidates with whom discussions can be opened. Having eliminated the obvious 'non-starters' and 'time wasters' they might well be reviewed against the checklist below:

- Define each candidate's business to determine whether the company's goods fit into their product range and activities.
- Assess each candidate's standing in terms of their existing principals and products and their relative market share (is the principal list too long, or dominated by an inividual principal?).
- Decide whether the candidate is accessible in terms of proximity to ports and commercial centres.
- Establish the financial status of each candidate from company reports (where they exist) or use agencies such as Dunn & Bradstreet. It would

13

not be advisable, however, to take up references at this stage.

- Try to establish some idea of the candidate's performance for existing principals. This might be done by observing how well their principals' products are distributed, displayed and serviced in the market. A more detailed study will obviously be necessary during the final selection stage.
- Examine the candidate's product range to see whether it points to experience in working with advertised products and involvement in sales promotion.

Screening short-listed candidates

The second stage of the screening process should take place in the territory itself. A short list of between three and five candidates should be visited in their offices.

The following checklist serves as a guide to the in-depth screening of short-listed candidates.

Investigating the distributor

- What is the visual impression of offices, warehousing, etc.?
- Can the distributor sell? Market check, meet salespeople, etc.?
- Can the distributor provide references from a large manufacturer for whom they act?
- Can they show a successful track record in similar products?
- Do they carry conflicting lines?
- Will they product their cost structure?
- How professional are they in marketing and sales methods?
- Can they provide an efficient after-sales service and do they appreciate the need for such activity in marketing terms? Do they provide such a service for other principals?
- Will there be any communication problems, i.e., can both parties communicate in the same language?
- What communication facilities does the candidate have – telephone, telex, competent clerical staff, etc?

Above all, are the distributor's staff the sort of people company management can get along with?

Screening of the salesforce

- How many salespeople does the candidate have?
- How are they divided?

- Do any have particular assignments (e.g. key accounts)?
- How are salespeople selected?
- What is the turnover of sales staff – how long do they stay?
- What has been the sales progression?
- How are sales staff trained?

Screening marketing staff

- How are marketing staff selected?
- What are their educational standards?
- How/where were they trained?
- Are they familiar with modern marketing methods? Are they intellectually committed to marketing problem-solving?
- Look at an example of marketing projects for other principals.
- Staff turnover – does the company train young managers and can it keep them?

General agreement of terms

Before entering the final discussions, it is a good idea for the candidate not only to be in general agreement with basic terms offered by the company but also to understand fully what service is required. This is the stage where a meeting of minds and a will to strike accord is all important. If you want the best distributor, dictating terms at this stage will put negotiations into a conflict situation, when what is needed is a desire to resolve matters to mutual advantage.

The following list covers the basic terms on which the company and distributor must agree.

- Stockholding requirements.
- Payment terms.
- After-sales service facilities (stockholding of parts).
- Advertising agency (which the principal may wish to appoint).
- Complaints procedures.
- Damaged/obsolete stock – write-offs.
- Staff training.
- Guarantees on products.
- Management of advertising and promotional funds.
- Stock/sales returns required.
- Margins and commissions.

13

The general agreement of terms will be somewhere between what the company wants and what the potential distributor is going to hold out for. A level of commitment needs to be shown by both sides at this juncture if the appointment is to have a genuine chance of benefitting from long-term cooperation. The agreement will form the basis of a distributor's contract. It is a good idea, however, when a verbal understanding is reached, to write a letter of intention to the distributor outlining the general agreement of terms.

Appointing the distributor

The final negotiations will be based upon putting the general agreement into specific conditions. In particular, the financial and stockholding terms should be thoroughly discussed, with both parties fully understanding each other in this respect.

Indemnities and termination

These matters must be discussed and, ideally, the candidate should be allowed to raise them. Mutual termination agreements should be included in the contract – and they must be potentially effective!

At this stage references should be taken out from the candidate's banks and one or two other principals.

Drawing up the contract

Items which should be included are:

- the name and address of each party,
- an agreement by each party to act to the best of their abilities in each other's interest,
- a description of the product to which the agreement applies,
- a concise description of territories covered by the agreement and a clause prohibiting selling operations outside the boundaries of the territories scheduled,
- the nature of the distributorship (exclusive or non-exclusive) and the areas of operation in which the distributor may, or may not, act as the principal's agent,
- the rights of each party in the agreement, including houses, accounts, special commission, rebates, etc.,
- the management of advertising and marketing funds,

- conditions to safeguard commercial security (brand names, patents, etc.),
- limitations on the distributor's rights to handle competing products,
- clauses to prevent the distributor changing, adulterating or spoiling the products by unauthorised repacking,
- the obligation on the distributor to provide an after-sales service as well as stocking spares, etc. The degree of responsibility that the distributor has in meeting claims, honouring guarantees,etc.,
- the duration of the agreement and the terms by which it can be cancelled or renewed, and
- the arbitration agreement.

Legal advice should be sought in preparing an agreement in the country where the distributor is located, and it must be made clear under whose law the contract is valid in both parties' countries.

Motivation and development

Once a distributor is signed up and begins operating on the firm's behalf, too many companies simply sit back waiting for the orders to roll in. There are three major considerations which need management's attention and professionlism if good distributors are to be entrusted with the full development of a market's potential:

- motivation and
- support and training of the distributor; and
- mutual commitment to build market.

The only way to keep a good distributor is to work closely and well with them, so that they can make money on your line of goods.

View your business from the distributor's side. Distributors must make money for themselves. If that automatically makes them earn money for you too, fine; but if they do not make a profit any good distributor will quickly drop your product. Regardless of personal relations, in which so many export salespeople seem to put so much trust, it is sale and profit that is of prime interest to a distributor. In motivating a distributor, by all means invite them to head office, make them feel important just as the books suggest, but make sure that they are making money on the company's products first.

Even though we have emphasised the point of the distributor making money, this is not something that can be simply ordained. Very often in fact, in the writer's experience, the distributor has to be pressed into making a success of the principal's product. By their very nature,

13

distributors have a polyglot inventory, amongst which they have to share time and resources. Demand pull on the inventory helps the distributor considerably. It means that the salesforce can work more quickly because there is market demand for the products. Unfortunately, when a company is newly represented in a virgin market, demand is slow initially. In fact, there is a high probability that the product will fail to achieve much in the way of volume for some time. This exacerbates the supplier's problems by the fact that the distributor is likely to be somewhat cautious in the introductory phase of its new principal's business.

Thus, we have a situation where initial demand will probably be slow. Extra attention will be needed on the new product range by the distributor and resources will have to be diverted. Inventories will, at the outset, tend to be modest and the distributor will be unlikely to overstock the trade. Here the problems occur, because if a proper marketing-oriented launch takes place, demand will create stock-outs quickly and there will be insufficient local stock holding to maintain demand. Hence the product will lose impetus in the market, leaving a gap for competitor activity. If entry is too cautiously planned, then demand is uncertain and this feeling may well prevail for some considerable time until either the products succeed or are withdrawn.

Motivation then, in the short term, surrounds the level of enthusiasm and confidence the company can create amongst the distributor's management and salesforce. A well-planned launch with high distribution objectives, coupled with a realistic communications programme, will help ensure success for the company, with a commitment to matching resources in terms of sales personnel and to the holding of sufficient stock.

The idea that distributors can become demotivated is one which often is not considered. If we adopt the general view that motivation is greatly diminished by disincentives of one kind or another, then we are unlikely to see the distributors highly motivated if the supplier presents a constant problem to them.

There are five probable factors which upset distributors most:

- The inability to process orders because of the principal's poor logistics system.
- Arguments over stock replacement.
- The danger that they may lose the business in which they have invested time, money and commitment.
- Parallel importing from other companies, either with the knowledge of the principal or because of the principal's international market pricing differences.
- Interpersonal strife between the two organizations can have a damaging effect on both relationships and business. (If conflicts cannot

be resolved, the managers involved will need to be dealt with by senior management on both sides.)

It is important for senior management to reinforce the management of distributors. This should be done by ensuring that any factors likely to lead to distributor dissatisfaction (especially in service areas) are reduced by sound organisation. Distributors are customers of the most loyal kind and should be treated as such. Urgent attention should be given to legitimate complaints and a truthful dialogue should be maintained regarding all matters of correspondence, particularly in processing orders and advice on delays of shipment.

Finally, it is vital to remember that the distributor's time is shared. Every other principal should be seen as a *competitor* in terms of using the distributor's time and energies. It is, therefore, imperative to keep reminding the distributor of the company's products and this can be achieved in the following ways:

- Make visits regularly.
- Write, send mailshots, and make reasons for communication, e.g. sending monthly stock availability reports and the company's annual report, creating a distributor's newsletter – anything which draws their attention to the company's products.
- Hold symposiums on a regional or global basis for new product introductions. The advantages of having such meetings to discuss advertising, sales promotion, new product instructions, and so on usually outweigh the disadvantages (some executives often fear the prospect of some distributors getting together after hours to compare prices, discounts and logistical support).
- Go to the distributor's sales force meetings and personally motivate the staff.
- Invite all key members of the sales staff over to your head office and let them view your factories, etc.

13

Support and training

As has been stated, it is necessary to provide a constant level of communication with distributors. This should be a two-way activity in matters relating to day-to-day business and also the long-term development of the market. Support not only includes the logistics function but should also involve maintaining adequate supplies of suitable catalogues (for sales staff and for direct mailshots to trade, etc.), samples and demonstration kits, as well as up-to-date, relevant literature from the trade press, research, special studies and, in the case of pharmaceuticals, up-to-date clinical studies and academic papers. Back-up also includes involvement and advice on direct marketing activities. Professional support in terms of advertising and promotional planning ensures not only that the company has a certain amount of control over its activities, but also that adequate time and care had been taken over marketing investment decisions.

Training is an essential activity which, because of its short-term cost against its longer-term payout, tends to be something which is constantly put to one side. Training programmes should be implemented to make sure that the distributor is fully conversant with the technical aspects of the company's products and, more importantly, their sales stories.

Never assume that every salesperson can sell. Some so-called sales managers may themselves have great difficulty in handling even a simple sales negotiation. The basics of selling may have to be revised, or even introduced, and there is no better teaching platform than the company's products. Add to this training on merchandising, distribution and special problems on handling the companies products, as well as the sales objections imposed by buyers.

One very useful training exercise which can be carried out regularly with numerous advantages is a sales staff discussion on buyer objections. A sympathetic forum or problem-solving discussion can, through an interchange of ideas, overcome many of the problems the salesforce has in gaining distribution of company products. It also gives executives a chance to lead and influence their distributor's salesforce, as well as giving them a greater insight into the dynamics of a particular market.

The need for salesforce incentives, special training, competitions, etc. are essential additions to the motivational practice of the company. An effective newsletter, regularly distributed, is a useful aid in reinforcing the dynamism of the company and its interest in the personnel of the distributor.

Above all, you must not be stingy in matters such as paying for training of staff and going beyond your legal warranty obligations to your distributor – they go beyond their legal warranty towards their customers, and they expect the same from you.

Mutual commitment to build the market

Nothing is more damaging to working relations than a feeling on the distributor's behalf that the principal is not committed to the market. One distributor in the tiny Mauritius market once said to the writer, 'I have just resigned a major Swiss pharmaceutical principal because he will not do anything out here. Okay, so we are a peanuts market, but if he wants to be here he should show some commitment'.

Should such a situation arise, the company must decide whether or not it wants to be in a market. If it does, then it should put in the necessary level of commitment to fully exploit its potential, and distributors should reciprocate. It is not an infrequent policy of distributors to hold on to a principal merely to prevent others from getting the business.

Parties should decide the point at which profits will begin to acrue. There is a tendency for exporters and distributors to begin milking profits too early, with the result that market penetration suffers, brand sales are stifled, and openings are offered to competitors.

The major threat for any distributor is that when business has developed to a significant size, the principal will cut loose and set up on their own. Many business people suspect, quite reasonably, that distributors hold back business for this very reason. Ideally, the progress and development of a market should involve the distributor. Distributors fear the loss of their business but it makes sense for them to become involved in projects such as contract manufacture and joint ventures in marketing or production. In fact, many well-organized distributors have the means and expertise to facilitate such extensions to their business. If, therefore, the distributor is involved with the development of a market and goes along with the principal, then business growth and mutual commitment are satisfied.

The common element in excellent distribution

The common element in successful principal – distribution relationships is a committed individual within the latter's organisation. They are, invariably, close to the market-place. Whether sales managers or sales-people, they are invaluable to the relationship. Through them impetus is given to the sales operation.

Such an individual is someone who, given the task of handling a principal's business, does so with enthusiasm and skill. A distributor may be obliged to recruit or train such a person to fulfil this role. Successful distributors will often do so without much prompting for a large principal. The alternative is for the company to locate a sales manager or representative within the distributor's operational shell, pay their salary, provide a car or car allowance and treat them as a company employee. For pharmaceutical companies and others with technical products which need personal detailing and demonstration, the employment of a representative is a must – particularly in competitive fields. With

13

marketable products, such people pay for themselves very quickly and provide companies with a competitive sales attack.

Changing poor performers

It is an uphill struggle to improve a poor distributor. One American company, 'Caterpillar', has a reputation for going against such an opinion. They will work so effectively with a distributor that they can make them good in many cases, but for most other companies, this method is too costly. There is then a trade-off between continuing to support a weak or bad distributor as a high opportunity cost and the cost of firing the distributor against the loss of business which will accrue should they be kept.

Changes should be made quickly, cleanly and thoroughly. No doubt the distributor will be somewhat emotional about the idea, but the benefit is more business through a more efficient agent. An active, changing distributor list produces more sales and tends to keep the average performers doing their best.

Moving from one distributor to another may have its short run problems. Trade customers may find it difficult to locate goods and the old distributor's stock has to be disposed of. There are dangers within the change-over period that stock-outs of important items will occur, thus leading to loss of market share. Service facilities may also suffer, leading to dissatisfaction among existing users. The biggest problem will, however, be the cost of cancelling a distributor's contract. In retrospect many executives find that cancellation clauses in the distributor's contracts should have been stronger. Had they been so, lengthy and expensive legal arguments could have been avoided.

It is well advised that prior to signature, cancellation clauses should be vetted by lawyers in the distributor's own country to minimise any local indemnification requirements to distributors upon cancellation. Naturally, having strong cancellation clauses in a contract is one thing, selling the idea to a new distributor is another. However, it is certainly worth holding out for, even at the cost of compromise in other aspects of the agreement.

Methods of doing business in certain countries affect the indemnity against distributors on contract cancellation. In Germany there is no indemnity against distributors unless they are commission agents with certain reporting obligations.

In France too, if a distributor is obliged to reveal names and addresses of purchasers, then the indemnity risk increases to compensate the distributor for information on the market which they have supplied – given that the information was not common knowledge in the first place.

There is no doubt that the laws covering principal–distributor relations vary considerably from country to country, and that these need to be studied separately for each new contract. Rarely are cancellation of contracts sudden and impulsive decisions. They tend to be arrived at as the conclusion is drawn from an appraisal of the distributor over a fairly long period. Financing cancellations can thus be budgeted for in fiscal planning in the same ways as other forecasted expenditures, e.g. stock write-offs, replacing obsolete equipment, or failed advertising films.

Finally, there is often a reluctance to avoid the issue of cancellation of distributor contracts because of cost and the personal unpleasantness of the task. However, the opportunity cost in terms of missed sales and profit opportunities should be the overriding factor. Executives may be putting themselves on the firing line because they are not producing results and if the factor is weak distributors then, as in any other aspect of their business, they should be obliged to solve their problems, even at the price of being called ruthless. Few managers can, economically or in terms of personal performance, tolerate weak, non-performing distributors in their areas of accountability.

13

14 Framework for an export plan

The framework □ The planning sequence □ Capital expenditure plan □ Strategy to fund expenditure □ The export plan document □ Conclusion

To conclude this book, I offer you a useful framework for developing an export plan. It aims to be a checklist for action – around which you build up your objectives, select products and markets, and create projects and market entry strategies.

It is a good idea to write a plan. Not only will this provide you with a working document for the future but the very process of constructing your paper will in itself help crystallise your thoughts and priorities.

Ideally your plan will involve other members of your team, with or without the counsel of a consultant. You might better delegate it to whoever is to champion your export development: give someone ownership of the project.

It must be stressed, however, that your export plan should be a central feature of your long-term business strategy – if it is to provide a major benefit to your business in terms of:

- Improving your competitive position.
- Providing new opportunites to develop your enterprise.
- Initiating a longer term international strategy.

It would be a waste of an opportunity to confine your export development to someone in the 'corner office'. It must involve all the functions of your business for, whilst markets may be managed and sales transacted by people assigned to them, you have to remember that the resultant business will call upon these resources:

- Production/warehousing
- Central administration
- Financial

The consequences of creating new business may lead to short-term problems with production, marketing investment and resources for the home market. If you are to be successful and gain fully from the benefits of your export markets, such problems must be planned for. Commitment to the cause and an enthusiastic response from managers and staff (whose workload may well be increased) needs to be encouraged.

The framework

One of the simplest ways to begin any planning process is to construct a framework around which the plan can evolve. Figure 14.1 provides a useful starting point.

The plan begins with the overall objectives you set: these are translated into market/product objectives. You should then look at your resources and discover what needs to be added to match your strategy requirements. The extent to which you need to scale up resources or modify your objectives will be one of the first decisions you will need to make. This decision will be easier if you put your plan into a time frame of, say, three to five years. This allows you to:

- Develop market and product projects, and forecast resultant volumes and revenues.
- Plan your resource development and capital expenditure plan over a period of time.

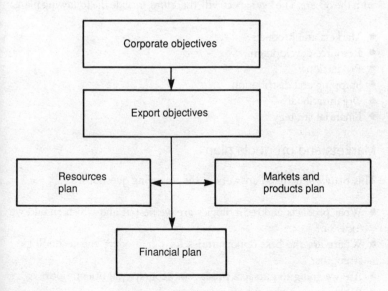

Fig. 14.1 Framework for an export plan

- Plan your financial strategy to match the needs of your market development and resourcing strategies.

The planning sequence

You can divide your planning framework into six stages, namely:

1. Decide on the direction of your plan in terms of the areas of business you intend to focus on, i.e., the technology you aim to exploit and the markets at which you are aiming your strategy.
2. Assess your own competitive position from an analysis of your firms strengths and weaknesses and the success criteria you need to establish to become successful.
3. Seek out your competitive advantages in terms of the market segment niches you are aiming at and whether you are offering uniqueness, flexibility or cost advantages.
4. Set objectives – business development, organization performance, time scales.
5. Evaluate your options against your constraints and set priorities.
6. Create projects.
7. Implement strategy.

Each element of your plan needs to be thought through and balanced with the others. The key aspect will, therefore, include the following plans:

- Markets and products
- Resource development
- Production
- Shipping and distribution
- Organisational
- Financial strategy

Markets and products plan

This plan will demand answers to the following questions:

- What products and technologies are we best at and which should we focus on?
- Where are the best opportunities for our product and technological strengths?
- Are we going to pursue a product or geographical orientation?
- Where can we obtain best prices?

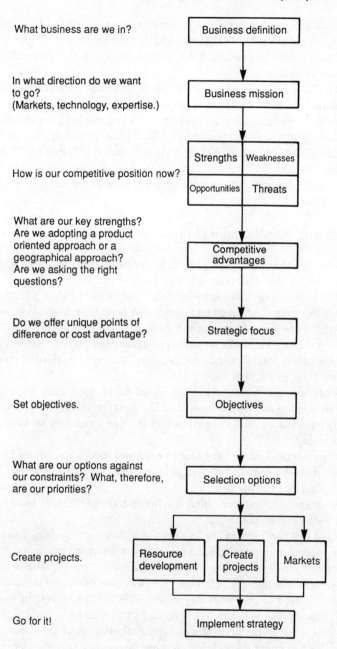

Fig. 14.2 Planning sequence

- What are the hurdles we will have to cross in terms of business environment issues, barriers to trade, distribution structures, etc?
- What product adaptations, R & D and technology applications will we have to consider?
- Which methods of market entry are we considering – direct sales/agent distributor, joint marketing venture, etc?
- Do we work from our own resources or do we employ a consultant?
- What grants are we eligible for – Enterprise Initiative, i.e. Design Initiative, Marketing Initiative, Export Initiative? (Contact DTI for information.)
- What are our objectives and expectations? How do these translate into projects?

Resource development plan

- What is the status of our present resources (production, innovation, marketing, financial, people, skills – ideas!)?
- Which weaknesses are a major constraint? Can these be put right quickly or are they structural issues which need to be worked on over time? If the latter, how long will it take?
- Are we located in the best place – production, head office, marketing/sales offices, warehouses, etc? Measure this against relative costs, proximity to markets, etc.
- What are our future objectives in terms of production capacity, warehousing and distribution, R & D output, marketing investment, organisation and skills requirements? By how much will we have to increase these?
- What resources do we have which we will not need in the future? How can these be disposed of and how, in financial terms, can they be recycled into the business?
- What special constraints limit our future course of action? How can these be surmounted?
- What are the risks to the business of either not matching market development or creating an over capacity or too many resources? Is it riskier to over resource or under resource? What are the relative cost penalties of either risk? How easy is it to dispose of surplus resources?
- Do we need to do everything in-house? What can be bought in or contracted out? What are the time horizons for each?
- What is the payout period for each project? How do we avoid the risk of the maximum costs (before revenue is generated) of each project falling together?
- How will the resourcing plan have to be financed – from revenue, share capital, joint venture, borrowings?

Production plan

- What are the key products and core technologies which will be focused on over the next few years?
- What are the volumes involved and how does this compare with our capacity?
- What are the minimum production capacity increments we can make? How much do they cost and how long will they take to bring on-stream?
- How do production costs behave with increases or decreases to volume output?
- What are our critical production constraints? How do we surmount them?
- Is our production located in the right place for minimizing costs, proximity to lines of distribution, proximity to markets?
- What are the benefits of moving production to export territories or spinning off export specials to contract producers, assembly operations, etc?
- What are the cost and capacity advantages of making in-house, buying in or contracting out?
- Is our production organised to exploit economies of scale or flexibility (which strength do we focus on)?
- Does our production plan match our strategic focus, i.e. uniqueness of our products, flexibility or low cost strategies?
- What is the gap between our capacity and capabilities and the needs of the export products and market plans?
- What production projects do we need to initiate and how long to completion?

Shipping and distribution plan

- What type of products do we have and what is the best and most suitable warehousing arrangement? A central warehouse or sub-warehouse nearer to ports or in markets?
- What sort of production planning and logistics system do we need?
- What sort of production lead times, product inventory, number of specials, etc., do we have to carry?
- What sort of distribution organisation do we need to meet customer service and marketing requirements?
- To which markets are we sending goods? What are the most effective, efficient and suitable methods for our overseas customers? Is there a special product requirement – hazardous cargo, refrigeration, etc?
- How will we provide a customer with order status reports?

14

- How will we tie the movement of goods and documents together?
- Will we use in-house expertise or contract out our distribution, shipping and documentation functions?
- How well do we know and use our forwarding agents? How many do we use? When was the last time we asked them to re-pitch for the business?
- How well do we understand and use insurance?
- What projects do we need to set in place and when will they be concluded?

Organisational plan

- Are we pursuing a geographical or a product oriented export strategy? Have we checked our assumptions that led us to the choice of strategy?
- What organisation do we have in place and how appropriate is it to our orientation?
- What skills and human resources do we have – market knowledge, languages, export experience? What resources will we need to buy in? What functions are best contracted out?
- Who will champion the export project?
- How will the internal management evolve? Will we go for a separate export department or not? (Product orientation possibly not the best route – geographical orientation probably the most appropriate.)
- How do we approach the problems of building on external organisation?
- Which methods of external organization are best for our business, our company culture, and are suitable for our products in selected markets – direct sales, export house, distributor agent, joint marketing arrangement, joint venture, etc? What would be our preferred method and how do we begin the process of locating partners?
- What projects need to be initiated to begin the process of developing an internal and external organisation.

Financial strategy

Only when you have looked at all the various planning elements can you begin to evolve a financial strategy. There are four aspects to it:

- The export business plan or budget (1–5 year profit/loss forecast).
- Capital expenditure plan.
- Funds flow projection.
- A strategy to finance the export development plan.

Years 1 – 5

	1	2	3	4	5
Sales *less* cost of goods					
Gross margin					
Less promotional marketing costs					
Profit contribution after marketing					
Less selling costs,					
administration costs,					
distribution costs					
Net contribution to profits					
Less financial costs					
Net contribution before below-the-line costs and incomes					
Plus royalty (income)					
Less licence fees (costs)					
Plus special commissions income					
Less special commissions costs					
Net contribution to profit					

Fig. 14.3 Export budget (1–5 year profit/loss forecast)

Special points to watch, however, are:

- Cost of goods – where volume increases are an essential element in improving overall company profitability, your cost accountant must examine the behaviour of costs in relation to volume changes. If this job is done sloppily, you will either overstate or understate your gross margin forecasts.

- Overhead costs in general administration, marketing/sales and distribution must not be double counted. At this stage in developing your plan it is probably worth discounting existing fixed costs (as they are already absorbed) and adding only incremental fixed costs to the calculations.
- Special incomes and costs such as royalties on licences or payments of licence fees, special commissions, etc. have been put 'below the line' in our example. This separates them from the main costs, and contributions from operations.
- You can apply whatever key ratios you use in your business to measure the monetary impact of the financial forecast on your profitability – e.g., return on investment, sales to contribution ratios, function costs to sales ratios, etc.

Capital expenditure plan

This plan will follow your normal and chosen way of planning your capital expenditure. The points to remember, however, are:

- The timing of commitments and their effects on funding requirements as payments or stage payments fall due.
- Separate the incremental costs of the export plan from those of the general needs of the business. If you have to build a new factory anyway, it is only the share of production that is destined for export which is put into the capital expenditure plan for the export development plan.
- Amortisation of costs should be based on your general policies for depreciation as this will impact on your profit/loss forecast.
- There has to be some trade off between the demand for expenditure and your financial constraints. Your strategy to finance the export development plan should address:
  - commitment to expenditure
  - timings of payments
  - the impact on the revenue forecast at both gross margin level (overhead costs) and at the finance cost level (costs of raising finance and funding).

Strategy to fund expenditure

If you are forced to under-resource your export business because you have not found a strategy to fund it, three problems occur:

- You will limit development to the speed attainable by available funds.
- Profit contribution will be difficult to reach as long as the business is operating below the level that makes it competitive in cost and price.
- You will be put in a position of 'forcing out' profits before the business matures, thus compromising its development.

You need, therefore, to examine your options to:

- Meet working capital requirements.
- Adjust policies for long-term borrowings and overdrafts.
- Look at options for raising additional share capital and measure their impact on your investors' attitudes (in terms of dilution of capital, earnings per share, dividend policy, control of the business, etc.).
- Look at options for joint venture financing in individual territories (the benefits of funding start-up costs from a joint venture have to be weighed against the same issues as those for raising share capital).

The other aspects of your financial strategy will, of course, concern:

- Risk management – risks inherent in project and market performance, foreign exchange transactions, buyer default, etc.
- Organisational issues – to control the financial aspects of your foreign business in terms of control, resources, skills training and so on.
- Financial reporting, policing and decision making will need to be embodied into your overall methods of operation. Remember that foreign business multiplies the complexity of running a company. You will need, therefore, to create a set of internal disciplines to prevent this complexity from creating major organisational and financial constraints.

The export plan document

Your export plan document is a business plan. Whether you are going to use it for external presentation or not, it is worth producing. The very task of preparing it means you will have thoroughly examined your opportunities and options. You will have quantified them and focused on the ways to tackle constraints. What is more, you will probably have learned a lot from it in terms of:

- Understanding your business.
- Exposing opportunities and threats.
- Testing the abilities of your people.

14

One example of the impact on a company which undertook this exercise was that it discovered that its production costing disciplines were grossly inadequate. The exercise above created considerable extra profit by forcing the financial management to completely overhaul its production costs. It suddenly found it had a lot less constraints than it thought to make substantial marketing investment both at home and abroad.

Conclusion

I hope you have found this book useful. The rewards of becoming an international business are tremendous. Yet it will be your initial approach which sets you on track for making a 'step change' to your future prospects. No doubt, if you have managed to follow the ideas in the text, you will appreciate the opening statement, that companies with a vision to become international have the propensity to do a lot better than those which do not, not just because of the enlarged business opportunity, but because of the attitudes and cultures of the people who are driving the business. If this culture can be assimilated by the entire work-force, your business will be driven by the dynamo of personal commitment, pride in running the business, and the kick they get from seeing their endeavours translated into success.

When one of my clients won the Queen's Award for Exporting after only 4 years of becoming an active exporter, it was in 46 countries and more than 70 per cent of sales were outside the UK. Now it has that little emblem to emblazon on its stationery and latest company report, as well as an enviable profit performance and balance sheet.

Exporting is one of the cornerstones for developing an international business. Through the international experience and networks of contacts it brings, it provides a whole wealth of opportunities for acquisition, joint ventures and corporate development. The time is right to enter 'Active Exporting' now.

Appendix 1:   The export plan document

Part 1

Evaluation of the Company – Its Opportunities and Threats

1.0 A general statement of directions and intentions against the general state of the market.
1.1 Outline of company strengths and weaknesses and a statement of success criteria needed to implement an export strategy.
1.2 A statement of your target market segments or niches and your chosen strategy (uniqueness, flexibility, cost) to exploit them.

Part 2

Objectives

2.0 A statement of objectives in terms of business development, organisation and financial performance. This will include both stated and quantified objectives.

Part 3

Options Priorities Projects

3.0 An outline of options and priorities.
3.1 An outline of projects in place or to be initiated. (Market research, market selection, market entry projects.)
3.2 Action plan for project implementation.

Part 4

Organisation

4.0 An outline of your internal organisational structures (product or geographic orientation).

4.1 A stated *first option* for overseas marketing, distribution service (and production).
4.2 An outline of alternative organisational options by territory.
4.3 An outline of organisational development projects.

Part 5

Production Logistics

5.0 Outline of production requirements in terms of products, special adaptions, volumes and capacities.
5.1 An outline of the production plan to include location, rationalisation for achievement of volume scale.
5.2 A rationale for spinning off parts of the production processes to contractors, buying in of components, locations abroad, packing, assembly, full production.
5.3 A statement on warehousing policy and outward logistics.
5.4 A list of production and logistics projects.

Part 6

A Timing Plan

Part 6 sequences the beginning and targetted end points of all key projects.

Part 7

Market Entry Plans

7.0 Target markets.
7.1 Methods of entry.
7.2 Marketing/production plan.
7.3 Methods of organisation.
7.4 Timings.

Appendix 2: Checklist for market entry projects for each market

1.0 Business Environment
- Economy, demography and competition
- Social and cultural considerations (urban or rural populations)
- Technological development
- Political, legal factors
- Barriers to trade

1.1 Taxation/Duty
- Import duty
- VAT
- Discriminatory taxes
- Withholding taxes on remittances of royalties/licence fees, etc.
- Personal taxation

2.0 Attractiveness of Market
- Estimate value, risk, attractiveness of market. Identify market segment, question the impact of social, cultural and legal barriers to trade for product adaption requirements and methods of market entry.

2.1 Legal Issues
- Price control
- Patents/copyright
- Agent/distributor contract (regulations protecting contracting parties)
- Anti-trust regulations
- Nationals only policies
- Advertising
- Terms of sale/price maintenance, etc.
- Product liability issues
- Legal advisors at home and abroad
- Foreign exchange controls
- Remittances of royalties/licence fees, etc.

2.2 Risk
- Market

- Contracting party
- Documentary credits/open account
- Credit insurance

2.3 Infrastructure
- Roads, railways, energy, social security, etc.
- Channels of distribution
- Communications
- Promotional infrastructure media, communication organisations
- Incentives and support (aid links)
- Banks and lines of credit
- Availability of distributors, agents, collaboration partners, etc.

3.0 Best Options for Market Entry
- Constraints
- Options – Direct export
         – Agents/distributors/export houses
         – Joint marketing arrangements
         – Joint ventures
         – Licensing

4.0 Pioneering Activities
- Making contacts
- Trade missions/joint venture exhibitions
- Grants and subsidies
- Visiting prospects/selecting partners

5.0 Marketing Mix Requirements

Product – Needs for adaption or modification, product function, styling, packaging, etc.

Place – Distribution system, distribution channels, target customers, service levels, coverage, controls

Price – Pricing policy, penetration or premium, margins, competition

Promotion – Target audience, available media, cost, competitive spend, advertising, PR, sales promotion, direct selling

6.0 Details of Launch Proposals
6.1 Product Specifications

6.2 Distributor/partner appointment/contract terms/payment terms
6.3 Sales/Production Objectives
   - Short-term 1–3 years
   - Long-term requirements
   - Production capacity
   - Stock holdings at home/in market
   - Outline constraints
6.4 Shipping Policies
   - Air, sea freight
   - Insurance category
6.5 Marketing Programme
   (Implementation of marketing mix)
6.6 Financial Plan
6.7 Monitoring and Activity Management Plans
6.8 Timing Plan

Appx 2

Appendix 3: The Queen's Awards for export and technology

If there is one way to really establish your firm's credentials, it is through having the emblem of a Queen's Award on your stationery. Apart from the achievement, the honour lifts the status of a company and provides opportunities for publicity, staff motivation and material sent to investors. If you are a company based in the UK, Channel Islands or the Isle of Man and meet the necessary criteria, you can apply.

There are two Awards – Export and Technology.

The Export Award is given to companies who can demonstrate a sustained level of export growth. However, the actual value of export business is viewed relative to the size of the firm's overall (UK and export) business.

The Technology Award is given to firms who can demonstrate a significant advance in the development of technology or technology transfer.

The Awards are designed to encourage and recognise outstanding achievement in either field. They differ from personal honours in that they are given to a 'unit' as a whole – both management and employees working as a team. There is strong competition for both of these Awards. They are granted annually by The Queen on the advice of the Prime Minister who is assisted by an Advisory Committee. This includes representatives of industry and commerce, the trade unions and the engineering institutions. It is supported by two Subordinate Committees, one examining export applications and the other the technology applications.

The Awards are valid for five years and holders are entitled to fly the Award flag (or both flags if they score a double) at their premises. They can also feature the emblem on goods produced in this country, on packaging and office stationery, in advertising, and on articles given to employees – such as neckties, lapel badges, brooches, cuff links and tie-tacks.

Lists of Awards are formally published in a special supplement to the 'London Gazette' and give the opportunity for publicity. Further publicity can be gained from presentation ceremonies later in the year.

The Queen's Award for Export Achievement

While various factors are taken into account, including improved marketing organisation or new initiatives to cater for export markets and size of the unit's operations, a basic feature is that the unit must show a substantial and sustained increase in export earnings over three consecutive twelve-monthly periods. Firms with a sustained high level of exports over a longer period may also submit figures for consideration as a consistently successful exporter.

The Queen's Award for Technological Achievement

Units are required to show a significant advance, leading to increased efficiency, in the application of technology to a production or development process in British industry or the production for sale of goods which incorporate new and advanced technological qualities.

An Award is only made when there is evidence that an innovation has achieved commercial success.

The R & D expenditure involved and the rate of return on this investment must be given.

The criteria

The full criteria and details of eligible activities are given in the notes with the application forms.

Who can apply?

Any organisation in the UK, Channel Islands or Isle of Man producing goods or services which meet the criteria is eligible for consideration. Individual persons are not eligible.

Neither the type or activity nor size or location of the unit influences the assessment. Apart from industry and commerce, research associations, educational establishments and similar bodies, as well as central and local government undertakings with industrial functions, are eligible for the Technology Award if they can show they have contributed to industrial efficiency through improved technology. (*Courtesy of the Queen's Award Office.*)

The benefits

A number of companies have seen the 'corporate' value in winning one of these Awards and have actually targetted achievements to qualify. No doubt winning the Award ahead of a 'stock exchange' listing or a 'strategic placement' can have quite a significant effect on prospective investors.

Appx 3

Appendix 4: Useful addresses

Embassies

Afghanistan
31 Prince's Gate
London SW7 1QQ
01 589 8891

Algeria
54 Holland Park
London W11 3RS
01 221 7800

Angola
c/o 5th floor
87 Jermyn Street
London SW1Y 6JD
01 839 5743

Argentina
49 Belgrave Square
London SW1X 8QZ
01 235 3777

Austria
18 Belgrave Mews West
London SW1X 8HU
01 235 3731

Bahrain
98 Gloucester Road
London SW7 4AU
01 370 5132

Belgium
103 Eaton Square
London SW1W 9AB
01 235 5422

Bolivia
106 Eaton Square
London SW1W 9AD
01 235 4248

Brazil
32 Green Street
London W1Y 4AT
01 499 0877

Bulgaria
186–188 Queen's Gate
London SW7 5HL
01 584 9400

Burma
19a Charles Street
London W1X 8ER
01 499 8841

Cameroun
84 Holland Park
London W11 3SB
01 727 0771

Chile
12 Devonshire Street
London W1N 2DS
01 580 6392

China
49–51 Portland Place
London W1N 3AH
01 536 9375

Colombia
3 Hans Crescent
London SW1X OLR
01 589 9177

Costa Rica
93 Star Street
London W2 1QF
01 723 9630

Cuba
167 High Holburn
London WC1V 6PA
01 240 2488

Czechosiovakia
25 Kensington Palace
Gardens
London W8 4QY
01 229 1255

Denmark
55 Sloane Street
London SW1X 9SR
01 235 1255

Ecuador
3 Hans Crescent
London SW1X OLS
01 584 1367

Egypt
26 South Street
London W1Y 8EL
01 499 2401

El Salvador
Flat 9, Welbeck Street
London W1M 7HB
01 486 8182

Ethiopia
17 Prince's Gate
London SW7 1PZ
01 589 7212

Fiji
34 Hyde Park Gate
London SW7 5BN
01 584 3661

Finland
38 Chesham Place
London SW1X 8HW
01 235 9531

France
58 Knightsbridge
London SW1X 7JT
01 235 8080

Gabon
48 Kensington Court
London W8 5DB
01 937 5285

East Germany
34 Belgrave Square
London SW1X 8QB
01 235 9941
West Germany
23 Belgrave Square
London SW1X 8PZ
01 235 5033
Greece
1a Holland Park
London W11 3TP
01 727 8040
Guatemala
13 Fawcett Street
London SW10 9HN
01 351 3042

Holy See
54 Parkside
London SW19 5NF
01 946 1410
Honduras
47 Manchester Street
London W1M 5PB
01 486 3380
Hungary
35 Easton Place
London SW1X 8BY
01 235 4048

Iceland
1 Eaton Terrace
London SW1W 8EY
01 730 5131
Indonesia
38 Grosvenor Square
London W1X 9AD
01 499 7661
Iran
27 Prince's Gate
London SW7 1PX
01 584 8101
Iraq
21 Queen's Gate
London SW7 5JG
01 584 7141

Republic of Ireland
17 Grosvenor Place
London SW1X 7HR
01 235 2171
Israel
2 Palace Green
London W8 4QB
01 937 8050
Italy
14 Three Kings Yard
Davies Street
London W1Y 2EH
01 629 8200
Ivory Coast
2 Upper Belgrave Street
London SW1X 8BJ
01 235 6991

Japan
43–46 Grosvenor Street
London W1X OBA
01 493 6030
Jordan
6 Upper Phillimore
Gardens
London W8 7HB
01 937 3685

South Korea
4 Palace Gardens
London W8 5NF
01 581 0247
Kuwait
45–46 Queen's Gate
London SW7 5HB
01 589 4533

Lebanon
21 Kensington Palace
Gardens
London W8 4QM
01 229 7265
Liberia
2 Pembridge Place
London W2 4XB
01 221 1036

Libya
119 Harley Street
London W1N 1DH
01 486 8387
Luxembourg
27 Wilton Crescent
London SW1X 8SD
01 235 6961

Mexico
8 Halkin Street
London SW1X 7DW
01 235 6393
Mongolia
7 Kensington Court
London W8 5DL
01 937 0150
Morocco
49 Queen's Gate
Gardens
London SW7 5NE
01 581 5001

Nepal
12a Kensington Palace
Gardens
London W8 4QU
01 229 1594
Netherlands
38 Hyde Park Gate
London SW7 5DP
01 584 5040

Somalia
60 Portland Place
London W1N 3DG
01 580 7140
South Africa
Trafalgar Square
London WC2N 5DP
01 930 4488
Soviet Union
13 Kensington Palace
Gardens
London W8 4QX
01 229 3628

Appx 4

Spain
24 Belgrave Square
London SW1X 8QA
01 235 5555

Sudan
3 Cleveland Row St
James's
London SW1A 1DD
01 839 8080

Sweden
11 Montagu Place
London W1H 2AL
01 724 2101

Switzerland
16–18 Montagu Place
London W1H 2BQ
01 723 0701

Syria
8 Belgrave Square
London SW1X 8PH
01 245 9012

Thailand
29–30 Queen's Gate
London SW7 5JB
01 589 0173

Togo
30 Sloane Square
London SW1X 9NE
01 235 0147

Tunisia
29 Prince's Gate
London SW7 1QG
01 584 8117

Turkey
43 Belgrave Square
London SW1X 8PA
01 235 5252

United Arab Emirates
20 Prince's Gate
London SW7 1PT
01 581 1281

United States
24 Grosvenor Square
London W1A 1AE
01 499 9000

Uruguay
48 Lennox Gardens
London SW1X ODL
01 589 8835

Venezuela
1 Cromwell Road
London SW7 2HW
01 584 4206

Vietnam
12–14 Victoria Road
London W8 5RD
01 937 1912

North Yemen
41 South Street
London
01 629 9905

South Yemen
57 Cromwell Road
London SW7 2ED
01 584 6607

Yugoslavia
5–7 Lexham Gardens
London W8 5JU
01 370 6105

Zaire
26 Chesham Place
London SW1X 8HH
01 235 6137

Commission of the European Communities

Commission of the
European Communities
8 Storey's Gate
London SW1P 3AT
Tel: 01 222 8122

(Information Unit)
11th Floor
Millbank Tower
London SW1P 4QU
Tel: 01 211 7060

Commission of the
European Communities
Winsor House
20th Floor
9–15 Bedford Street
Belfast BT2 7EG
Tel: 0232 240708

EC Centres for European Business Information

Centre for European
Business Information
Small Firms Service
Ebury Bridge House
2–18 Ebury Bridge Road
London SW1W 8QD
Tel: 01 730 8115

Birmingham Chamber
of Industry & Commerce
75 Harborne Road
Birmingham B15 3DH
Tel: 021 454 6171

Newcastle Polytechnic
Library
Ellison Building
Ellison Place
Newcastle NE1 8ST
Tel: 091 232 6002

Strathclyde Euro
Infocentre
Scottish Development
Agency
25 Bothwell Street
Glasgow G2 6NR
Tel: 041 248 7806

European Business
Information Centre
Irish Export Board
Merrion Hall
PO Box 203
Strand Road
Sandymant
IRL Dublin 4
Eire
Tel: 0001 353 169 5011

uropean Business
nformation Centre
hannon Free Airport
Development Co
he Granary
Michael Street
RL Limerick
ire
el: 0001 353 614 0777

uropean Community
ME Task Force
ue d'Arlon 80
040 Brussels
elgium
el: 010 322 236 1676

usiness Corporation
entre
C Net
ask Force on Smes
ue d'Arlon 80
040 Brussels
elgium
el: 010 322 230 3948

EN
ue Brederode 2
TE 5-1000
russels
elgium
el: 010 322 519 6811

ENELEC
me as CEN above

merican Chamber of
ommerce
 Brook Street
ondon W1Y 2EB
el: 01 493 0381

ustrian Commercial
elegate in Great
itain
Hyde Park Gate
ondon SW7 5ER
el: 01 584 4411

lgo-Luxembourg
amber of Commerce
 Great Britain
ohn Street
ndon WC1
l: 01 831 3508

Canada-United
Kingdom Chamber of
Commerce
3 Regent Street
London SW1Y 4NZ
Tel: 01 930 7711

French Chamber of
Commerce
Knightsbridge House
197 Knightsbridge
London SW7 1RB
Tel: 01 225 5250

German Chamber of
Industry & Commerce
12–13 Suffolk Street
London SW1Y 4HG
Tel: 01 930 7251

Italian Chamber of
Commerce
Walmar House
296 Regent Street
London W1R 6AE
Tel: 01 637 3153

London Chamber of
Commerce and Industry
69 Cannon Street
London EC4N 5AB
Tel: 01 248 4444

Netherlands British
Chamber of Commerce
Dutch House
307–308 High Holborn
London WC1V 7LS
Tel: 01 242 1064

Norwegian Chamber of
Commerce
Norway House
21–24 Cockspur Street
London SW1Y 5BN
Tel: 01 930 0181

Portuguese Chamber of
Commerce and Industry
New Bond Street House
1–5 New Bond Street
London W1Y 9PE
Tel: 01 493 9973

Spanish Chamber of
Commerce
5 Cavendish Square
London W1M 0DP
Tel: 01 637 9061

Swedish Trade Council
73 Welbeck Street
London W1M 8AN
Tel: 01 935 9601

Entra
8-6673116
8- 6629989
1 FAX

Association of British
Chambers of Commerce
Sovereign House
212a Shaftesbury
Avenue
London WC2H 8EW
Tel: 01 240 5831

8-6635280

Association of British
Factors
Moor House
London Wall
London EC2Y 5HE
Tel: 01 638 4090

FAX
8-66274 57
Federation of Swedish
(Commerce med
In portes

British Export Houses
Association
69 Cannon Street
London EC4N 5AB
Tel: 01 248 4444

British Institute of
Management
Management House
Cottingham Road
Corby
Northamptonshire
NN17 1TT
Tel: 0536 204222

British Overseas Trade
Board
1 Victoria Street
London SW1H 0ET
Tel: 01 215 3520

Overseas Fairs and
Outward Missions
Dean Bradley House
52 Horseferry Road
London SW1P 2AG
Tel: 01 212 0093/6277

Appx 4

BOTB Regional Offices

Industrial Development
Board for Northern
Ireland
IDB House
64 Chichester Street
Belfast BT1 4JX
Tel: 0232 233233

West Midlands Regional
Office
Ladywood House
Stephenson Street
Birmingham B2 4DT
Tel: 021 632 4111

South West Regional
Office
The Pithay
Bristol BS1 2PB
Tel: 0272 272666

Industry Department
New Crown Building
Cathays Park
Cardiff CF1 3NQ
Tel: 0222 824171

Industry Department for
Scotland
Alhambra House
45 Waterloo Street
Glasgow G2 6AT
Tel: 041 248 2855

Yorkshire &
Humberside Regional
Office
Priestley House
Park·Row
Leeds LS1 5LF
Tel: 0532 443171

South East Regional
Office
Ebury Bridge House
Ebury Bridge Road
London SW1W 8QD
Tel: 01 730 9678

North West Regional
Office Sunley Building
Piccaddilly Plaza
Manchester M1 4BA
Tel: 061 236 2171

North Eastern Regional
Office Stanegate House
2 Groat Market
Newcastle upon Tyne
NE1 1YN
Tel: 0632 324722

East Midlands Regional
Office
Severns House
20 Middle Pavement
Nottingham NG1 7DW
Tel: 0602 506181

British Standards
Institution
(Technical Help to
Exporters)
Linford Wood
Milton Keynes
MK14 6LE
Tel: 0908 320033

Central Office of
Information
Hercules House
Westminster Bridge
Road
London SE1 7DU
Tel: 01 928 2345

Confederation of British
Industry
Centre Point
103 New Oxford Street
London WC1A 1DU
Tel: 01 379 7400

Council for Small
Industries in Rural
Areas
141 Castle Street
Salisbury
Wiltshire SP1 3TP
Tel: 0722 336255

Croner Publications
Croner House
173 Kingston Road
New Malden
Surrey KT3 3SS
Tel: 01 942 8966

Crown Agents
4 Millbank
London SW1P 3JD
Tel: 01 222 7730

Department of Trade &
Industry
Ashdown House
123 Victoria Street
London SW1E 6RB
Tel: 01 212 7676/3395

(Exporting Licensing
Branch)
Millbank Tower
Millbank
London SW1P 4QU
Tel: 01 211 6611

Design Council
28 Haymarket
London SW1Y 4SU
Tel: 01 839 8000

Export Credits
Guarantee Department
Aldermanbury House
Aldermanbury
London EC2P 2EL

ECGD Regional Offices

River House
High Street
Belfast BT1 2BE
Tel: 0232 231743

Colmore Centre
115 Colmore Row
Birmingham B3 3SB
Tel: 021 233 1771

1 Redcliffe Street
Bristol BS1 6NP
Tel: 0272 299971

72–80 Hills Road
Cambridge CB2 1NJ
Tel: 0223 68801

Welsh Office
Crown Buildings
Cathays Park, Cardiff
CF1 3NQ
Tel: 0222 824100

Sunley House
4 Bedford Park
Croydon
Surrey CR9 4HL
Tel: 01 680 5030

Fleming House
134 Renfrew Street
Glasgow G3 6TL
Tel: 041 332 8707

West Riding House
67 Albion Street
Leeds LS1 5AA
Tel: 0532 450631

Clement House
14–18 Gresham Street
London EC2V 7JE
Tel: 01 726 4050

Elisabeth House
St Peter's Square
Manchester M2 4AJ
Tel: 061 228 3621

HM Customs and Excise
King's Beam House
Mark Lane
London EC3R 7HE
Tel: 01 626 1515

Institute of Directors
116 Pall Mall
London SW1Y 5ED

Institute of Export
World Trade Centre
St Katharine's Way
London E1 9AA
Tel: 01 488 4766

Institute of Freight
Forwarders
Suffield House
9 Paradise Road
Richmond
Surrey TW9 1SA
Tel: 01 948 3141

Institute of Marketing
Moor Hall
Cookham
Maidenhead
Berkshire SL6 9QH
Tel: 06285 24922

Institute of Patent
Agents
Staple Inn Buildings
London WC1V 7PZ
Tel: 01 405 9450

Institute of Practitioners
in Advertising
44 Belgrave Square
London SW1X 8QS
Tel: 01 235 7020

Institute of Public
Relations
1 Great James Street
London W1N 3DA
Tel: 01 405 5505

Institute of Trade Mark
Agents
69 Cannon Street
London EC4N 5AB
Tel: 01 248 4444

International Chamber
of Commerce
(British National
Committee)
Centre Point
103 New Oxford Street
London WC1A 1QB
Tel: 01 240 5558

Licensing Executives
Society
Registered Office Only:
33–34 Chancery Lane
London WC2A 1EW

Overseas Press and
Media Association
(OPMA)
122 Shaftesbury Avenue
London W1
Tel: 01 734 3052

Paper and Board,
Printing and Packaging
Industries Research
Assoc. (PIRA)
Randalls Road
Leatherhead
Surrey KT22 7RU
Tel: 0372 376161

Simplification of
International Trade
Procedures Board
(SITPRO)
Almack House
26–28 King Street
London SW1Y 6QW
Tel: 01 930 0532

United Nations
(London Information
Centre)
14–15 Stratford Place
London W1N 9AF
Tel: 01 629 6411

Information
Sources and
Databases

Celex (EEC) Spearhead
(DTI)
Accessible through
Profile Information
Telecom Gold
Mercury Link Electronic
Mail Service
One to One

British Library Business
Information Service
25 Southampton
Buildings
Chancery Lane
London WC2A 1AN
Tel: 01 323 7454

Appx 4

British Library
Document Supply
Centre
Boston Spa
Wetherby
West Yorkshire
LS23 7BQ

Market Research and Intelligence

CTA Economic &
Export Analysts Ltd
96 London Road
Reading RG1 5AV

Market Research Society
175 Oxford Street
London W1R 1TA
Tel: 01 439 2585

A C Nielsen Co Ltd
26 High Street
Kidlington
Oxfordshire
Tel: 08675 71759

Technical and Legal Advice

Technical Help to
Exporters
British Standards
Institution
Linford Wood
Milton Keynes
MK14 6LE
Tel: 0908 220022

British Institute of
International and
Comparative Law
17 Russell Square
London WC1B 5DR
Tel: 01 636 5802

Brebner & Co
107 Cheapside
London EC2V 6DT
Tel: 01 600 0885

Consultants

Ernst & Whinney
Becket House
1 Lambeth Palace Road
London SE1
Tel: 01 928 2000

James Dudley
Management
22 Copperfields
West Wycombe Road
High Wycombe
Buckinghamshire
HP12 4AN
Tel: 0494 25385

Anvil Dexter Ltd
Marketing and Sales
Training
(Highly recommended
for Exhibition training)
18 Belton Drive
West Bridgford
Nottingham
Notts NG2 7S1

Technology

Eureka Office
Room 204
Ashdown House
123 Victoria Street
London SW1E 6RB

British High Commissions

Antigua & Barbuda
38 St Mary's St, PO
Box 383 St Johns
Australia
Commonwealth
Avenue, Canberra
ACT2601
Bahamas   Bitco
Building, East Street,
PO Box N7516,
Nassau

Bangladesh   Abu Bakr
House, Plot 7, Road
84, Gulshan, PO Box
6079, Dahka 12
Barbados   Lower
Collymore Rock, St
Michael, PO Box 676,
Bridgetown
Belize   Embassy
Square, PO Box 91,
Belmopan
Botswana   Queen's
Road, Private Bag
0023, Gaborone
Burnei   Hong Kong
Chambers, Jalan
Pemencha, PO Box
2197, Bandar Seri
Begawan 2085
Canada   80 Elgin
Street, Ottowa,
Ontario K1P 5KT
Cyprus   Alexander
Pallis Street, PO Box
1978 Nicosia
Dominica   (as
Barbados)
The Gambia   48
Atlantic Boulevard,
Fajara, PO Box 507,
Banjul
Ghana   Osu Link, Off
Gamel Abdul Nasser
Ave., PO Box 296
Accra
Grenada   14 Church
Street, PO Box 56, St
George's
Guyana   44 Main
Street, PO Box 10849,
Georgetown
Hong Kong   Bank of
America Tower, 12
Harcourt Road, GPO
Box 528, Hong Kong
India   Shantipath,
Chanakyapouri, New
Delhi 110 021
Jamaica   Trafalgar
Road, PO Box 575,
Kingston 10

Kenya   Bruce House,
Standard Street, PO
Box 30133, Niarobi

Kiribati   Bairiki, PO
Box 61, Tarawa

Lesotho   Linare Road,
PO Box 521, Maseru

Malawi   Lingadzi
House, Capital City
Centre, PO Box
30042, Lilongwe 3

Malaysia   Wisma
Damansara, Jalan
Semantan, PO Box
11030, 50490 Kuala
Lumpur

Maldives (as Sri Lanka)

Malta   7 St Anne
Street, PO Box 506
Floriana

Mauritius   King
George V Avenue,
Floreal, PO Box 186
Curepipe, Port Louis

Nauru   (as Fiji
Embassy)

New Zealand   2 The
Terrace, PO Box
1812, Wellington 1

Nigeria   11 Eleke
Crescent, Victoria
Island, PMB 12136,
Lagos

Papua New Guinea
Kiroki Street,
Waigani, PO Box
4778 Boroko, Port
Moresby

**St Christopher and
Nevis**   (as Antigua
and Barbados)

St Lucia   Columbus
Square, PO Box 227,
Castries

St Vincent   Granby
St4reet, PO Box 132
Kingstown

Seychelles   Victoria
House, PO Box 161,
Victoria, Mahe

Sierra Leone   Standard
Bank of Sierra Leone
Building, Lightfood
Boston Stree,
Freetown

Singapore   Tanglin
Road, Singapore 1024

Solomon Islands
Soltel House,
Mendana Avenue, PO
Box 676, Honiara

Sri Lanka   Galle Road,
Kollupitiya, PO Box
1433, Colombo 3

Swaziland   Allister
Miller Street,
Mbabane

Tanzania   Hi fadhi
House, Samora
Machel Avenue, PO
Box 9200, Der es
Salaam

Tonga   Vuna Road,
PO Box 56,
Nuku'alofa

Trinidad & Tobago
Furness House, 90
Independence Square,
PO Box 778, Port Of
Spain

Tuvalu   (as Fiji
Embassy)

Uganda   10–12
Parliament Avenue,
PO Box 7070,
Kampala

Vanuatu   Melitco
House, Rue Pasteur,
PO Box 567, Vila

Western Samoa   (as
for New Zealand)

Zambia   5210
Independence
Avenue, PO Box
50050, Lusaka

Zimbabwe   Stanley
House, Stanley
Avenue, PO Box
4490, Harare

Appendix 5: Bibliography

Kotler, P.   *Marketing Management*, 5th edition. Prentice Hall International Inc., 1984.

Dudley, J.W.   *1992 Strategies for the Single Market* Chartered Institute of Management Accountants and Kogan Page, 1989.

Dudley, J.W.   *Successful Exhibiting*. Kogan Page, 1989.

Dudley, J.W.   *How to Promote Your Own Business*. Kogan Page, 1980.

Dudley, J.W.   *The Directors Guide to Choosing and Using an Advertising Agency*, Chapter 10. The Director Publications, 1985.

Porter, M.E.   *Competition in Global Industries*. Harvard Business School Press, 1986.

Porter, M.E.   *Competitive Advantage*. The Free Press, 1985.

Index